All Aboard !

To Jan

ALL ABOARD!

Around Britain With Help From My Friends

ROD SHIERS

To Richard,

best wishes

Rod Shiers

Lodestar Books

Published 2015 by
Lodestar Books
71 Boveney Road, London, SE23 3NL, United Kingdom

www.lodestarbooks.com

A CIP catalogue record for this book
is available from the British Library

ISBN 978-1-907206-34-4

Typeset by Lodestar Books in Equity

Route charts drawn by Claudia Myatt

Printed in Spain by Graphy Cems, Navarra

All papers used by Lodestar Books
are sourced responsibly

Contents

The Route

Acknowledgments

Many people have assisted me in writing this book I am grateful to Simon Beckett and my friends at Bakewell Writing Group for all their advice and encouragement, and to Helen Dalton for copy-editing. As to the adventure which gave rise to the book I couldn't have managed without Dave Marshall's unstinting help in preparing Shearwater and his keeping faith with me, despite our early setback. Thanks are due to the friends and relatives who joined me on the trip and put up with my eccentricities. Last of all a special thanks to my wife Jan, who has tolerated my sailing for so many years and made it all both possible and worthwhile.

One

࿇

'WE'RE GOING TO LOSE IT,' shouted Dave. The mast swayed before plunging backwards to crash into the sea on our port side. What had been a neatly rigged sailing yacht, with her mainsail boomed out to capture the following breeze, was now just a tangled mass of ropes, steel cables and mangled guard rails. What had been an exhilarating sail up the North Devon coast was suddenly a struggle to avoid being washed up amongst the surf of Bude. What had been, a week ago, my first adventure in *Shearwater*—to deliver her from Poole to Portishead—was ending in disaster.

The boat was wallowing in rolling seas, drifting dangerously close to shore. The swish of spray glancing along the hull, the rhythmic creaking of cabin fittings, the straining of ropes, the familiar sounds of sailing—all had deserted *Shearwater*. She lay quietly in the water as though awaiting retribution for placing us in this predicament. The new, unwelcome sound was that of the mast, at its foot still secured to the boat by the remnants of cables and ropes, clanking on the outside of the hull, threatening to punch a hole through the fibreglass and welcome in the cold, grey sea.

'We're not going to get it back on board. It's too heavy,' I shouted. A few months earlier I'd watched a documentary of a staged dismasting, which had set out to see what six strong men could achieve, for them only to fail and be forced to cut the mast free. There were two of us, and hardly in our prime. I studied the rigging cables, straining under their load, sawing backwards and forwards across the top of the cabin and gnawing cuts into the top of the gunwale. If I got out the hacksaw and set to, I wondered which of them would spring up and garrotte me. 'I think we're going to need some assistance,' I yelled.

Dave started the engine and tried to manoeuvre the boat to keep the mast clear of the hull. I scrambled into the cabin, performing a limbo under the crushed spray hood frame, and gripped the VHF radio mike. How many times had I practised this in the classroom, I thought? What level of distress message should I send? It hardly mattered. There would be no marks awarded, only 'pass' or 'fail.'

'Mayday, Mayday, Mayday. Yacht *Shearwater*, Yacht *Shearwater*, Yacht *Shearwater*. My position is...' I reeled off our position then added, 'Approximately five miles south west of Bude. We have been dismasted and require assistance...'

As I waited for a response I remembered my aged mother's reaction when my brother had first told her of my plans to sail around the UK: 'What's he want to do that for at my time of life?' I'd laughed when I'd heard, but perhaps she was right. Perhaps there were safer and more sensible projects to undertake in retirement. The idea was originally born out of the need to have an answer to a stock question posed in the run up to my escape from the world of work: 'How do you intend to use your time?'

At first I trotted out pithy rejoinders like, 'Oh, just monitoring my pulse, watching the weeds grow. That sort of thing.' But these weren't satisfying, least of all to me. Sailing around the UK sounded bold, exciting and intrepid, the antidote to slippers and a mug of cocoa. It wasn't long before I'd told enough people of my plans that I felt obliged to convert them into reality.

It wasn't that outlandish. I'd been sailing most of my life, even after moving from my childhood home on the shores of the Thames Estuary, to what the journalists dub 'landlocked Derbyshire.' I'd discovered new sailing pals and dinghy racing on Ogston reservoir, near Chesterfield, but felt something was still missing—the tang of the sea. This particular itch was only finally scratched a few years later, after I was married with young children, when we bought our first offshore boat. I sailed her from the muddy creeks of Essex to a new berth at Dartmouth. During the next thirteen years, at weekends and during most holidays, I dragged the family up and down the M5 from Derbyshire to the River Dart. We explored the Devon coast and later crossed to the Channel Islands and Brittany.

When we outgrew that boat we bought a bigger, better one to share with some Ogston friends. Twenty years, three boats and a lifetime of Mediterranean exploits later, my half share lay in Croatia. Even if our boat partners had agreed to join in my plan it would have taken too long to bring our French yacht back to England, and she was the wrong sort of boat anyway. I needed a more traditional craft, one that could take the ground. For this trip I had no need of a bathing platform and stern shower, or any of the other trappings that seem essential for warm water cruising.

A long-standing friend at Ogston, who was a few years ahead of me in the retirement stakes, felt obliged to hang up his boots. Harry's boat, *Shearwater*, a Westerly Fulmar, seemed ideal for the trip. She is thirty two feet long, with twin bilge keels so she can stand on the bottom in a drying harbour. There was some work needed to bring her up to scratch but I felt she was the right yacht and, not long after my retirement party, she became mine. I planned to spend my first work-free winter re-fitting the boat. I planned to move her to Bristol, this being nearer to home and a good starting point for my big trip. I could use the passage from Poole to Portishead to re-acquaint myself with sailing in British waters and to get to know the boat. Of course, that was when she had a mast and sails. That was then, I thought, when it was all fresh and exciting...

I listened for a response to my Mayday call, but there was none. Hardly surprising, now that the aerial on top of the mast was out of sight under the waves. My mobile phone was showing one bar signal strength, and I dialled 999. Within seconds I was speaking to Falmouth Coastguard.

'You're in luck,' said the duty officer. 'Padstow all-weather lifeboat is already at sea. They can be with you in half an hour.' He must have sensed the tension in my voice, when he added, 'Are you alright, skipper?'

'Yes, we're fine. We have lifejackets, but no life raft.'

Ending the call, I climbed back on deck and handed Dave a lifejacket. 'The lifeboat's on its way. We'd better put these on. Don't want a lecture when they arrive.'

At that point there was a munching sound from the back of the boat and bits of chewed up foresail floated out from under the stern. With the engine running there was always a risk of us fouling the propeller on part of the rig, and that would have made matters much worse.

'We'll have to manage without it,' I said. Dave looked shoreward, shrugged and cut the engine. Silence again. It could have been peaceful apart from the elephant in the water. Perhaps, with hindsight, I shouldn't have tried to get the sails down when Dave first noticed the forestay had gone slack. Perhaps I should have run forward and rigged up a temporary stay, but who volunteers to perform the foxtrot around forty feet of heavy gauge aluminium, swaying in the breeze?

'Now what?' said Dave, jerking me back to reality. We could have spent the time rushing around the boat collecting tools and starting to clear away the wreckage, but a combination of lack of confidence and mind-numbing shock reduced us to just standing and staring, nervously scanning the beckoning shore and then the horizon to the south. The back stay was lying across a dent in the stern rail where it had been kinked in the impact. The spray hood was well and truly mangled. I shuddered to think of the consequences, had the mast fallen directly backwards into the cockpit.

I screwed up my eyes to squint long and hard back down the coast, and spotted a small dark smudge which grew steadily into the distinctive blue and orange livery of a lifeboat. She was steaming at high speed, her bow wave a flash of foaming white in the dark sea. The deep growl of powerful engines sank to an impatient grumble as she hove to a few metres off our bow. The coxswain, resplendent in bright yellow oilskins, stood in the high bridge structure. He cupped his hands and shouted across.

'Morning, need some assistance? What do you want us to do?'

I was tempted to say 'wind the clock back a few hours and help me check the forestay before I set out,' but decided against it. 'We can't recover the rig,' I cried. 'We could do with a hand to cut it away.'

He nodded and gave instructions to two of his crew who launched an inflatable dinghy and motored across. They climbed aboard and tied off to our stern.

'Been breaking things have we?' said one of them.

'We set out from Padstow this morning,' I replied. 'Having a lovely sail, before this. Now we've turned her into a gin palace.'

They laughed. 'Well this is a first for us,' one of them said. 'Let's start by disconnecting the rigging screws.'

Buoyed by their confidence we began to work with them to clear the rigging. In a careful sequence ropes and wires were cut through and bottle screws undone. One of the lifeboatmen went forward and sawed through the aluminium foil on the genoa roller furling tackle. He came aft and pressed a heavy boot on top of the last shroud fitting while his mate freed it off. With an irritable flick from the cable, like an angry snake lashing out, the mast and remains of the sails and rigging succumbed and slid silently beneath the waves.

'Now what?' I asked.

'Can you start your engine?' one of them said. I explained about the bits of sail and the possibility we had fouled the prop.

'We could head for Bude, it's close enough.'

'There's not much there and you don't want to be attempting the entrance in this sea. Best we tow you back to Padstow.'

He radioed the lifeboat, and the coxswain manoeuvred close enough for them to hurl a heaving line across, to which they had attached a bridle and a stout towline. When we were all secure the two lifeboatmen joined us in the cockpit for the long haul back to the Camel estuary, from where we'd started out six hours earlier. Even if our prop wasn't fouled we were probably making quicker progress under tow than we would have done with our puny engine. The lifeboat was at the limits of its area of operation and had already been out at sea for a number of hours. I suspected they preferred to be towing us at their speed rather than escorting us back at our pace.

Given the circumstances we had a good laugh on the journey back. The lifeboatmen were both ex-fishermen. They said they'd been out that morning trying to find a navigation buoy which had broken free in Canadian waters and had drifted across the Atlantic.

'More interesting helping you chaps,' one of them said. 'Sometimes you get some right cases. Last month we went out to a yacht which had run out of fuel. He had a spare can of diesel on board but said he didn't want to get his decks messy. We didn't sit with him on the way back; we went up on the foredeck.'

We took that to mean we were a worthy shout. One of them stared at a stool I'd knocked up to improve the view over the spray hood. He ran his hand over the woodwork. ''Andsome that is. 'Andsome.' It tickled us and we adopted the phrase for a time. After three hours we arrived back at Padstow, where the harbourmaster said we could lay alongside the waiting pontoon until we got ourselves sorted out. The lifeboat cast us off. It's hard to adequately express your gratitude in these situations. We simply shouted 'Thanks.'

After the relief of the rescue I had to force myself into action to tackle the resultant mess. I took photos of the damage for the insurance claim and examined the sawn off end of the roller furling tackle, expecting to see the stub of the forestay. There was nothing there. Somehow it must have become detached and I guessed that was what had brought about the dismasting. There were no repair facilities in Padstow and it was important to get the boat to Portishead, where I had booked a place in the yard for the planned re-fit. We were still over a hundred miles away. I'd read about the notoriously powerful tides in the Bristol Channel and although in theory we could have continued the passage under engine alone, I didn't fancy tackling it in a boat with no sails and mangled guard rails.

The night before we'd met a couple who put into Padstow with engine trouble. They peered over the breakwater wall and asked what had happened. For the first time we told the story. They were sympathetic and said it made their problem seem like nothing. They were probably right. After they had gone we resolved to keep the mishap to ourselves for as long as we could. Neither of us fancied reliving the experience time and again.

I phoned my wife, Jan and told her the news. She was shocked. 'Oh, Rod, are you both ok?'

My voice broke a bit. 'Yes, love we're fine.'

I didn't say much because I knew it could have been very different. But the fact was, no one had been hurt and the damage to the hull was minimal. The harbourmaster gave me the name of a boat haulier based across the estuary from Padstow, at Rock. I phoned him and he said he could lift *Shearwater* the next day and transport her to Bristol the following morning. This would at least mean the boat would be arriving at her destination on time, albeit not in the manner I had planned.

Two

❧

SHEARWATER PROBABLY COULD HAVE MANAGED to circumnavigate the British Isles with no more than a lick of paint. Some people say you just need a boat, three months to spare and simply cast off. But for me part of the adventure was the re-fit. I envisaged endless hours of fun during the winter months, to banish any nostalgia for drafting easements and shareholders' agreements. I needed to move her to a new berth, and choose my departure point. Any yachtsmen with a pint in hand will argue the merits of a clockwise route and vice versa. All I knew was that most voyagers have enjoyed better weather and longer hours of daylight in the Highlands in early summer so I resolved to arrive in those parts as early as possible. Bristol has a fine seafaring tradition and what more appropriate place from which to spring from my shackles of slavery?

So it was settled. I booked a place in the yard at Portishead Marina, and one blustery August afternoon in Poole harbour I sat proudly in the cockpit of *Shearwater*, as her new master, awaiting the arrival of my brother, Paul. I was pleased he could join me at the beginning of the delivery trip. He had accompanied me on my first offshore sailing trip twenty five years earlier. The boat then had been a Westerly of similar age to *Shearwater*. Someone had suggested it would have been easier and quicker to use a road haulier. This was true, but I needed the voyage to familiarise myself with the boat, and with sailing once more in British waters. For the previous fifteen years nearly all my offshore sailing had been in the Mediterranean where, apart from guessing the often unpredictable weather patterns, seamanship tends to consist of planning the next lunchtime anchorage and evening restaurant.

In the weeks before our departure I brushed up on my offshore sailing theory. Interpolation of tides, shipping forecast areas, VHF radio protocols, all washed back to occupy my waking day and interrupt my sleep. I wondered how

I would cope with all the detail. It sounded good when I was trotting out my plans, and my friends were impressed at the adventure of it all. But could I deliver?

The morning we left Poole the wind was blowing from the south-west Force 4 gusting 5, as Paul and I tacked *Shearwater* towards St Albans Head on the passage towards Weymouth. Sailors always say 'towards', not 'to': it's less embarrassing if you have to change destination. As we approached St Albans the waves began to crash over the bows and I realised we'd stood in too close to the headland and were caught up in overfalls. This term is jargon for the confused sea-state resulting from a strong tidal stream 'falling off' an elevated area of seabed. Overfalls will quite cheerfully toss a boat around and, if you're lucky, spit you out the other side. We scampered south into calmer water and, after a boisterous beat across Weymouth Bay, furled the sails and motored in between the breakwaters. OK, that was the first passage under our belts. I radioed the harbourmaster to request a berth for the night.

'Yacht *Shearwater*, no problem, but you'll have to raft up in the Cove alongside a red hulled yacht.'

I was puzzled. When I last sailed in England harbourmasters were a grumpy lot who considered yachtsmen a nuisance to the commercial shipping fraternity. Perhaps the Tourist Board had introduced a charm offensive. And I'd forgotten all about rafting up. This is the procedure for mooring your boat alongside another, and clambering over its deck to get ashore. There's a protocol to be observed which involves tiptoeing around your neighbour's foredeck and never through the cockpit where, who knows, the skipper's wife might be sunbathing topless. On their foredeck you must avoid staring into the fore hatch where more amorous activities might be in progress. It's a bit like the neighbours crawling over your conservatory to get to their car.

We managed to tie up alongside the red yacht without scratching her paintwork. A blue ensign fluttered from her transom, defaced with some sort of military insignia, probably an armed forces yacht club. Two burly crew were accompanied by a shapely young woman.

'Evening,' the skipper said. 'Where 'yer bound for?'

'Brixham,' I replied.

'It's the Solent for us. We'll be leaving to catch the first of the flood at six tomorrow.'

I remembered the tide, that god which governs all sailing passages in British waters. If the inside boat needs to leave everyone outside her has to re-moor.

'OK,' I said. 'No problem, we'll be up to take the lines.'

When we returned from our meal ashore they were sitting in the cockpit and invited us to join them for a night cap. At the end of a successful first day I was keen to soak up the camaraderie of like-minded sailors. Big mistake. The young woman dispensed drinks with the alacrity of a NAAFI bar steward on double bonus. Her efforts, and my folly, were compounded by my offer to share a bottle of single malt I'd brought along. The evening came to an abrupt end when I was obliged to lean over the side and feed the fish, before clambering unsteadily back on *Shearwater*. The next thing I remembered was waking in the middle of the night, cradling the porcelain bowl, with my knees wedged against the bulkhead. I crawled to my bunk. It seemed only minutes before I heard footsteps on the deck and a loud thump on our hatch cover.

'You're adrift at the stern,' a voice shouted. The red yacht was leaving.

At breakfast Paul eyed me suspiciously. I'm not known for my drinking and I could see him wondering if retirement had brought about a change of behaviour. Mercifully the direction of the tide dictated a late start for us, so I had a few hours to gather my senses, but my head was still pounding when we left harbour and set a course to clear Portland Bill. There was no wind, the sea was calm and we took the inside passage, close enough to hear the chatter of the sunbathers on the rocks. Portland is one of those major headlands where, in certain conditions, the surging tide of the English Channel trips up and creates massive waves. I was grateful for the flat water but could have done without the thump of the engine which accompanied us throughout the passage.

The crossing of Lyme Bay was uneventful but took all afternoon and most of the evening, and it was dark when we picked our way amongst the lobster pot buoys that littered the entrance to Brixham harbour. Ah, lobster pots, I thought, another reminder of home waters. They have them all over the world, but I've never seen so many unlit buoys obstructing the fairways as infest the waters of the English south coast. If you snag your propeller on one the only way out is to brave the cold sea and, armed with a serrated knife, slash your way free. If you're unlucky a fouled propeller could rip the shaft out of your boat and cause it to sink. We avoided this delight, and my radio call to the marina prompted some torch-waving and the arrival of the night berthing master, who allocated us a berth.

We woke the next morning to the sound of howling wind and rain. This was more like the weather I'd expected and was all prepared for. Paul helped me rig a tent over the cockpit. I'd made this at home, anticipating wet days when I could sit under cover splicing ropes and doing other yachty activities. The cover leaked along the seams but kept out the worst of the weather. *Shearwater* was fitted with an old enamel gas stove, which was efficient but frightened the life out of me. When the oven was on you could see the reflection of the burner flames dancing on the back of the housing. It all looked too open and there was no fail-safe so it was easy to knock a gas tap and turn it on accidentally. Despite all this it functioned and I cooked a hearty breakfast and we sat about in the cabin until we grew bored.

We put on our foul-weather gear and, looking like the washed up yachtsmen we were, wandered up to explore the town. Brixham is the oldest town in Tor Bay and once was home to the largest fleet of wooden fishing boats in the world. All that has seriously diminished but the harbour still bustles with life. The fishermen were unloading alongside the fish dock, and taking on ice and provisions before setting out to sea again. They seemed unconcerned by the gale keeping the yachtsmen skulking in harbour, or perhaps they had no choice. I bought a large golfing umbrella that looked tough enough to withstand a seaside storm.

Later in the day the rain eased and we strolled up to Berry Head. Peering over the cliff tops we saw a yacht making heavy weather through the choppy seas. We were glad it wasn't us. On the way back we hopped into the *Maritime Inn*, a classic old pub with enough bric-a-brac to sink a ship, and met Mr Tibbs the parrot. We slowly supped two pints of *Pheasant Plucker* (which truly is its name and not the test of how much you've consumed) and sauntered back to the harbour. After devouring a curry we joined the trippers for the firework display that nowadays seems obligatory at every seaside town in August. I supposed we were trippers really. We dropped a few coins in the collecting bucket.

The next day the forecast was still dismal. It was only twelve miles to Dart-mouth but having sailed out of this port for many years, our arrival was to be a sort of homecoming and I wanted to enjoy it in the best weather, not slink in soaking wet and feeling sea sick. We decided to stay another day in Brixham and ate breakfast in the refurbished restaurant built over the fish market. It's a mod-ern, trendy design, the gents' sporting urinals fabricated from galvanised buckets, with portholes overlooking the harbour. Very thoughtful.

In the evening we walked up to the marina office and studied the weather up-date, anxious to read some good news. After a couple of days in harbour you can get obsessed with the weather and some sailors develop cabin fever, a creeping lethargy that is only cured by a fair breeze and sun on your back. The forecast looked promising and on that note we retired to our bunks. The next morning a fair breeze was blowing, funnelling down the valley behind the town and pinning *Shearwater* against the pontoon. We had some fun getting off (a euphemism for cursing, shouting at each other and persuading a small single propeller yacht to reverse in a straight line). As we stowed the fenders Paul announced that in the excitement he'd lost his designer sunglasses. He seemed a bit hurt when I said I couldn't understand anyone paying megabucks for a famous brand name. He's always been the more stylish of the two of us.

In warm sunshine and a gentle breeze we savoured a lazy sail along the coast and soon enough arrived off the Mewstone, which lies at the entrance to the River Dart. On one shore stands a castle, on the other a stone tower between which they used to stretch a heavy chain cable to keep out the dastardly French fire ships. Nowadays English Heritage will rent out the tower to holiday makers, even the French. The wind dropped and we part sailed, part drifted on the flood tide past the Lower Ferry with its quaint pull-push tug, past Bayard's Cove, still looking as magnificently pristine as when it starred in *The Onedin Line* on televi-sion. It felt like only a few months, not tens of years, since our children whooped with delight as they hauled crabs from the river and waved at the steam trains puffing into Kingswear.

We picked up a mooring at Dittisham and joined the crowd for a pint in the *Ferryboat Inn*, overlooking the harbour. The place was heaving and was no quieter when we returned to eat that night. We waited hours for pie and chips and Paul's had to go back to be defrosted and cooked in the middle. It must be England on a bank holiday, I thought. Following our one day of sunshine the bad weather returned with a vengeance the next morning. In torrential rain we motored back down to Dartmouth where we rafted up on a visitors' pontoon in the middle of the river. I took the dinghy across to Kingswear and waved Paul off at the station. Later in the week my wife Jan joined the boat for the regatta celebrations. She doesn't trust me and when we go sailing takes her own weather. It was warm enough to eat lunch in the cockpit and snooze in the sunshine.

'It could almost be the Med,' she declared, which I took as faint approval. The next morning it was time for the first running repair. The genoa, the large foresail which rolls up when not in use, has a sacrificial covering strip along two edges to protect it from the sun when furled. This chose our present trip to complete its sacrifice, and had shredded. I lugged the sail bag along the narrow cobbled streets and left it with a sailmaker. It being regatta week, his loft was piled high with racing sails in urgent need of repair, and he was relieved when I said I didn't need it for a few days.

We drove home, so I could complete some domestic chores, and a few days later I met up with Dave, who was to crew for the remainder of the trip. We parked his van in Bristol, ready for our homecoming, and then caught the early morning train to Paignton. I shopped for provisions while Dave bought some tickets for the steam train to Kingswear. This was to be the highlight of his trip. Like many engineers, his enthusiasm extends beyond the demands of work to include all manner of mechanical devices, the older and more obscure the better. To Dave an old, rusty tractor is an object of beauty. He wore a grin the width of the carriage as we puffed along the Dart valley, the train pausing momentarily at the halt for the former Agatha Christie residence.

Back on board *Shearwater* the genoa had been repaired. We stowed our gear and hoisted the sails, and set off in time to catch the ebb tide around Start Point. It was good to be sailing again. The early September weather was friendly enough and a gentle breeze carried us past Salcombe and across Bigbury Bay to the River Yealm, one of my favourite overnight destinations. As I started the engine for our final approach, Dave announced his plans to catch our supper and proceeded to pay out a fishing line on a frame. It wasn't long before he recovered a tangled mess of orange line, accepted defeat and blamed the equipment.

'I need some better swivels,' he said.

'I bought a ready meal just in case,' I muttered.

The entrance to the River Yealm is hidden in the corner of Wembury Bay with rocks and a sand bar to trap the careless. Inside, the river deepens and winds between steep wooded hillsides. We motored up towards the visitors' pontoon, but were met by the harbourmaster who directed us to an unused local mooring. Much better. After dinner we sat in the cockpit, drinking coffee and listening to the last of the birdsong. When the damp chill of early autumn enveloped the cockpit we retreated to the cabin and took an early night.

The next morning we cast off at first light, eating breakfast under way. Our destination was Falmouth, fifty miles down the coast. The sea was flat calm and we had to motor all the way. The Bukh engine chugged away, puffing condensed exhaust vapour from the stern. I was wary of the engine, as it was original equipment and looked like it. My concern was as much about my ignorance of diesel engines. I've only ever changed the oil and checked the fan belt. But I knew Harry had lovingly cared for it and the more I talked to people in the know, the more I gained respect for Bukh, it being one of the few manufacturers to produce diesel engines specifically for marine use. I didn't want to slow the boat down for another fishing attempt, and as a consolation promised Dave a decent meal ashore. The engine didn't disappoint, and late in the afternoon we entered Falmouth Roads and moored at the yacht haven, within view of the Maritime Museum and the huge docks which dominate the harbour. Falmouth still distinguishes itself as a working port.

Not the least of the attractions in town is Trago Mills. No one can visit Falmouth without marvelling at this labyrinth of sales space stacked from floor to ceiling with every conceivable commodity at bargain prices. Dave decided it was the ideal place to purchase more sophisticated fishing tackle. Technical advice was a bit sparse, with comments from the sales assistant like 'we sell a lot of these,' but eventually he selected a sturdy rod and a 'professional' reel, costing a whole £4.50.

The next morning, before leaving harbour, we queued up at the fuel berth. On a sailing boat the trick is not to get stuck behind a motor cruiser (perhaps unkindly labelled by yachtsmen as a gin palace or gas-guzzler). If you are unfortunate you'll have to waste an hour while they take on a zillion litres of diesel and the skipper hands over the equivalent of the GDP of a third world country. We were first in the queue, ahead of a speed boat and had been enjoying some banter with its skipper.

'How much do you want, mate?' asked the fuel berth attendant.

'Twenty litres should do it,' I said.

'Not worth bothering is it?' came the retort from behind us.

As we left Falmouth there was a distinct absence of our preferred power source, so we put the trusty Bukh to work and motored past the Lizard, the most southerly point of the UK, and chugged across Mounts Bay. St Michael's Mount shimmered in the hazy sunlight, looking for all the world like a magical fairy castle. Dave was keen to try out his new fishing kit and I slowed the boat to a couple of knots. On his first cast the reel exploded into bits, revealing its sophisticated mechanism.

'I've never seen gear teeth made out of flimsy plastic,' I said. 'Still I suppose you only get what you...'

'Don't say it. Don't say anything.' He packed up his gear and I increased the revs.

'Meat pie tonight then, is it?' I said.

Penzance is the natural choice of harbour if you're planning to round Land's End, but its lock gate only opens for about three hours either side of high water. We had some tricky tidal calculations for the next passage and I wanted flexibility on our departure time, so we headed towards Newlyn. Until recently this harbour was strictly for fishing boats, but some pontoons have been installed to accommodate yachts if space permits. Space did permit and we moored up amongst the fishermen, who ignored us. The harbourmaster took our berthing fees and recommended a place to eat.

'Are there any showers?' I asked. He grinned and shook his head. After dinner we considered the next leg. The North Cornish coast has very little shelter, necessitating a passage of sixty miles to Padstow. You need certainty in the weather and some careful planning. First, you have to round Lands End, working the tides so you don't get swept onto the rocks guarded by Longships lighthouse. Then you sail forty miles up the coast to arrive at the River Camel with enough water to cross the sandbank at the entrance, optimistically called Doom Bar. At Padstow you must catch the opening times for the mechanical sill which keeps boats afloat in the harbour. The final approach is via a small creek with rocks on one side and a large sandbank separating it from the Camel estuary. The necessary calculations had us arriving at 2030, when it would probably be dark. Great, I thought, for a first visit.

The forecast the next morning was good apart from the threat of fog. For a small yacht there is nothing more intimidating than mixing it with large ships in poor visibility. I still shiver when I recall years ago traversing the shipping lanes of the English Channel one foggy day and hearing the sound of a ship's engine which we never saw, only its wake as we crossed. The promise of the weather clearing overcame our reticence and at 0600 we groped our way out of the harbour, dodging the lobster pots scattered like banana skins around the entrance. With such poor visibility our navigation needed to be spot-on, and meticulously we steered our planned course between the buoys, noting the distance to run between each and ticking them off in the log. Occasionally, through the grey mist, we caught a glimpse of the coastline. Mousehole fleetingly loomed like a scene from a ghost play, drifting into view before disappearing forever. After a couple of hours the sun got the upper hand and as we approached Lands End the fog cleared to reveal the famous headland, proudly jutting out into the Atlantic.

When Longships lighthouse appeared then slid behind us we shaped a course northwards up the Cornish coast. The promised south westerly wind never arrived and we motor-sailed all day, but the sun held out and at dusk the horizon was a deep crimson as we entered the Camel Estuary. There was just enough daylight to pick out the buoys leading to Padstow. It was dark as we drew level with the red lights guarding the harbour entrance. Another yacht was moored to a buoy in the deep water pool and we moored alongside until the harbour opened. They'd sailed from Milford Haven, and had engine trouble and were waiting for a tow into harbour the next morning.

When the entrance lights turned green we cast off and cautiously conned the boat along the creek. Dave stood at the bow, our spotlight bouncing off the rocks on our starboard hand. A face appeared over the harbour wall and directed us to a berth. I'd put the dinner on whilst we were waiting, and as we made fast the smell of supper wafted up from the cabin. We tucked into a good meal before dropping into a contented sleep. It had all been going quite well—at least until we lost the mast next morning.

Three

❧

M OST YACHTSMEN HATE SHOPPING, unless the shop in question is a yacht chandler. Even the most hardened salt will dissolve into gooey-eyed wonderment at the sight of shelves crammed with fittings and must-have gadgets to enhance the sailing experience. The yachtsmen's equivalent of London Fashion Week is the Boat Show. In January one can escape a dark winter's day, wandering along the broad aisles at the Excel Centre where, under bright lights, the dreams are of sunny days at anchor in a deserted cove sipping gin and tonic. The other big show takes place in September at Southampton. This is the final hurrah of the sailing season. Thoughts turn to the winter re-fit and the chance to snap up bargains.

It was to this event that Dave and I headed with a long shopping list. I had planned to use the passage from Poole to Bristol to discover what was needed to prepare for the big trip. Top of the list was a new chart plotter. This is a sailor's version of a satnav. For short coastal hops or sailing between the islands in, say, the Med, with no currents or big tides to speak of you, could get away without one. The charter boat briefing usually consists of 'Sail in the blue bits, anchor in the green bits and drink beer in the brown parts, and don't get them mixed up!' But sailing around the British Isles is another matter, and the system I inherited on *Shearwater* was more akin to a black and white TV.

I felt a responsibility to the crew and to my family to provide a liferaft, and we needed some good binoculars. And so it went on. If we weren't yet ready to buy we quizzed the experts and ran our hands over the display models. By the end of the day the credit card lay panting in my wallet and we staggered home with the car well loaded. I could hardly wait to open the boxes and drool.

My plans for the re-fit were coming together but there was the conspicuous absence of a mast and sails, and quite a few mangled bits. I travelled down to Portishead to meet the surveyor appointed by the insurance company. I was nervous in case I'd done something, or omitted something, which caused me to fall foul of the weasel words in the policy. Having to bear the cost of replacing the mast and sails could potentially scupper my plans altogether. I needn't have fretted. The surveyor was a decent guy, who had worked in the Westerly yards and knew the boats inside out. He could see from her cabin and hull that *Shearwater* was in good condition. He told me that roller furling gear was notorious for causing dismastings. We shook hands and he left me feeling confident that the claim would go through. I was greatly relieved.

Before leaving for home I went to find the marine engineer who works out of the boat yard. He operated from a unit rammed to the rafters with a jumbled mass of boat bits and half-finished work. I picked my way through and knocked on the office door. There was just room for me to step inside where I met Ray. His desk and every other surface was covered with boxes, paper and equipment. I tried not to stare at the wall and a revealing Pirelli calendar featuring a young lady who, I suspected, knew nothing about tyres, still less about marine engineering.

'I'm looking for someone to do some repair work on my Westerly, the one that arrived without its mast,' I said.

'Oh that one,' he replied. He didn't ask any more and I assumed he knew the back story.

'And I want to fit a powered anchor winch.'

We walked back to *Shearwater* and he studied the damage, making all the right noises. We pored over the catalogue of his main supplier, and Ray promised me the insurance quotes I needed. He said he could get all the work done by the following spring. On the drive home I pondered my choice of contractor. I had little doubt he could do all the work, but the state of the workshop and the constant mobile phone interruptions reminded me of chasing tradesmen with more customers than time to service them. In the sailing world, if you're not at the head of the queue during the winter the chances are slim that your boat will be ready for the new season.

Autumn turned to winter. Dave was approaching retirement and was keen to find a project. I gratefully accepted his offer to help with the re-fit. We spent a couple of days on the boat, doing odd jobs and making long lists. The most urgent job was making the cabin watertight. Tell-tale stains on the headlining revealed water was penetrating the deck. We slept on board but it was bitterly cold and we spent two miserable nights in the damp. Out of the water the hull lost the insulation of the sea and we resolved to sleep elsewhere on future trips. The final quotes were sent to the insurer, approved and orders placed before Christmas.

We were away for most of January and I spent the time planning the trip. I had read the experiences of several other voyagers and decided to aim to complete the trip in three and a half months. If I left in early May I could be home by mid-August in time to take Jan away for some summer sunshine. Having sampled warm weather sailing in the Mediterranean she wasn't enthusiastic about returning to chill British waters, but said if the weather and location sounded right she'd join me at some stage. I proposed to invite Ogston members and old sailing pals to join me for each leg, dividing the trip into week-long cruises.

There was work to be done, so early one morning in February Dave and I left the snow-clad hills of Derbyshire and drove to Portishead, where it wasn't much warmer. We sat in the warm fug of Dave's van building up the courage to dress in cold work gear and clamber on board *Shearwater*. Our first overnight accommodation was a soulless budget chain hotel, so after that each week I tried to find interesting guest houses at budget prices. The only stipulation was twin beds. You have to draw the line somewhere. On one outing we booked into a sprawling old place overlooking the Bristol Channel at Clevedon. We arrived on the first evening to be met by the proprietor, brandishing a large screwdriver.

'I'm really pleased with myself,' he said. 'I've been meaning to fix these doors for ages.'

We paced along the musty-smelling corridors to our room with a view, where we soon discovered plenty more potential uses for the proprietor's screwdriver, not least of all the shower head which came off in Dave's hand. On the first night we made the mistake of using the restaurant, where the chef seemed to favour a cuisine using only packets of dried food and grease. It was so cold in the room we swapped dining tables three times, progressing from the bay window to hard up against the tepid radiator. We decided to forego breakfast the next morning and went to check out. At the desk there was a buxom blonde with a mouth large enough for two. She was shouting that no one could get in or out of the main entrance. We recounted our arrival tale regarding the 'fixed' doors.

'I'll effing kill him when I get my hands on him,' she screamed. 'Can you fix this effing entrance?' The tools we needed were in Dave's van, the other side of the imprisoning doors, but with the aid of some cutlery we managed to prise our way out and escape.

A pattern was established. We'd drive to Portishead early one morning, work flat out for a couple of days and retreat home, where Jan would reward us with a tasty supper. On one trip I forgot to take my boat keys and borrowed the set I'd left with Ray. On the last evening we finished work and wearily walked to the washrooms to clean up before the drive home. He'd packed up before us so when I locked the boat I put the keys back through his letter box. Or thought I had until I tried to get into Dave's van. Not surprisingly, the boat keys didn't fit the van lock. Dave was pretty good about it. I phoned Ray who told me he lived about an hour away but I turned down his offer to return. I couldn't drag the poor guy out again. We were facing another night in a hostel but then I had an idea. The other engineers in the yard were still working.

'You don't happen to have one of those strong magnets, do you?' I asked. The guy in the yard nodded and produced a lump magnet on a rope, normally used to retrieve items accidentally dropped overboard. I threaded this through Ray's letterbox and began fishing. My first haul produced some rusty chain but eventually after scrabbling about I heard the chatter of light metal and much to my relief raised the van keys. That night the meal at home was even tastier and my bed even cosier.

Slowly the work took shape. Jan had requested that I replace the black toilet seat. I thought I could easily accommodate this request. Far from it. I ordered a new white seat, only to discover it was designed for the newer model of toilet. Needless to say I couldn't exchange it and embarked on a tedious battle to match existing fittings to what I had recently purchased.

The final insult came when I sold the redundant ceramic bowl and pump on eBay. The carrier must have dropped it because I received a caustic email from the buyer accompanied by a photo of smashed pieces of toilet bowl and a demand for a refund.

The arrival of spring did nothing to improve the miserable weather. It was often too cold to use adhesives and Ray rigged up a boat cover and heat lamps to dry out the deck. Each morning Dave and I would scrape the frost off the hatch cover before diving into the cabin to work on whatever would keep us out of the elements. Inside the cabin looked more like a workshop. The headlining was down, the cushions were at home and every surface was smothered with tools or part-completed projects. Sometimes we struggled to find a place to sit and drink hot soup. It was hard to imagine it ever looking like a yacht again.

At home I put the finishing touches to my invitation. I split the trip into week-long segments, some of short distance to allow for tarrying amongst the Scottish isles, and others longer, including the planned dash down the east coast. On the schedule that accompanied the invitation I marked two 'no sailing' weeks. The first of these, just three weeks in, would allow for any repairs to the boat or teething problems. The second week, after I hoped we would have arrived in Orkney, would allow me to return home to check that Jan hadn't sold the house. I set up the mailing list, and pressed the send button. It was a bit of a gamble, particularly sending it out to the entire club membership, some of whom I didn't know at all. I thought I might have to do some discreet organizing to keep known antagonists apart, but it all worked out well. Someone said he quite fancied one of the 'no sailing' weeks.

I got the expected range of responses. Most people just signed up, knew they'd be making their own travel arrangements and had no qualms over heading to join me in the more remote parts of the country. Others phoned with questions about ferry times and the like, none of which I was able to answer. I stressed to everyone that I wasn't operating a Cunard cruise, nor able to guarantee the pickup point. I could only promise a week's sailing on *Shearwater* somewhere in the British Isles that summer. I owed it to Dave to invite him on as many legs as he could make but, in typical unstinting fashion, he elected to come along for the first three weeks and then join me up in Orkney.

One old friend, Syd, wanted two consecutive weeks. He is a great character, full of stories, which he never exhausts because when he's told them once you get them again a few days later. He phoned me one evening with a question: 'Do I need to give up the pipe?'

Syd has a hardcore pipe-smoking habit. This involves cutting from a block a lump of sticky, tar-laden tobacco, which is lovingly packed into his pipe bowl. He then ignites the fuel and puffs contentedly, enveloping those around him in a blue haze of noxious smoke. I took his question to mean that if I replied, 'yes, no pipe' he would have declined to join me. I compromised and said I could only fit him in for one week. The crew list came together surprisingly easily. In addition to me there would be three crew for most of the legs. There was no turning back now. Holidays had been booked, transport arranged and expectation was running high. I just needed an improvement in the weather to enable me to finish the re-fit.

By the beginning of April it was still not warm enough to antifoul the hull. A big milestone was the day we stepped the new mast. Ray surveyed it laid out on trestles in the yard and said 'That's a big mast, I had to ring up to make sure they'd got it right.' I assured him it was correct. Fulmars were designed as performance cruisers. Westerly's original plan had been to use them for match racing. 'I've got a 40 footer but my mast isn't that tall,' he said. After that Dave and I would compete to be the first to point out the particularly tall mast in a harbour. Childish, I know.

With her mast stepped *Shearwater* once again resembled a yacht. Eventually the weak spring sunshine overcame the frost and, in the middle of the day, the temperature rose sufficiently to complete the heat-sensitive work. The sprayhood and guard rails appeared and were fitted and one morning awaiting our arrival in Portishead there was a large box containing two new sail bags. It was getting exciting. With this sort of project you can go on forever, always finding another small improvement to introduce. But I had a departure day and crew awaiting their slot. If I set off late there would be chaos from the start. I booked the crane for the following Monday, gave Ray the deadline and urged him to complete his work. Dave and I took to offering assistance, holding tools and generally making a nuisance of ourselves. Finally the anchor winch buzzed into life and a long length of shiny galvanized chain was measured out in the yard, then hauled aboard, complete with a new anchor.

On the day of the re-launch there was still a list of outstanding jobs. The deck painting was left to last and when the travel crane lumbered across the yard to sweep up *Shearwater* and gently lower her into the water we had to tiptoe across the deck to avoid the areas that were still tacky. The engine fired up and I remembered to 'burp' the water-lubricated prop-shaft bearing. This involves hanging upside down in the cockpit locker and squeezing the rubber shaft seal, like milking a cow, only you get sea water instead of milk. If you don't do it the shaft burns out the seal and the boat sinks. No big deal then.

We motored round to our appointed berth. It was great to be afloat. The next morning was bright and sunny with no wind, ideal for bending on the new sails. When we hoisted the genoa, (the large foresail), it proved to be too long to get the correct luff tension. It would have to go back to be re-cut, which was a nuisance because the following day we had planned to set out on our sea trials. We decided to go anyway, if only to try out the mainsail and the anchor winch. As it turned out there was no wind, and we just motored down the coast, anchored up, had lunch and motored back again. It was an anticlimax but at least the engine ran well enough, which was a relief after the cold winter layup. We returned home that night knowing the next visit would be to load the boat for departure. Not ideal, but we were just about ready.

I had a clear week before setting off.

'Would you like to go away this week?' I asked Jan. 'Anywhere you fancy, here or abroad. I'll be gone for three months.'

She paused for a few seconds. 'Well, I've got swimming on Wednesday and the hairdresser on Thursday.'

This put my trip into perspective. Her mum, on the other hand, clearly felt the undertaking was no trifle. When we took her out for Sunday lunch on the weekend before departure the innkeeper greeted me, 'Mrs Martin says this is your last lunch. Are you off somewhere?'

Four

❦

DAVE WAS WAITING AT OGSTON when I drove over to pick him up. It was a glorious spring afternoon.

'Let the adventure begin,' I said, which seemed appropriate. It was my birthday and I had invited a few friends for dinner and a send-off celebration. It was warm enough to have pre-dinner drinks in the garden, and the meal passed in excited exchanges about the plans ahead. I didn't sleep much and was glad when it was dawn. Dave and I set off early in my car, full to the brim with clothes and kit. My daughter followed on later with Jan. Arriving at Portishead, I was relieved to find the genoa had been returned from the sail makers and when we hoisted it the cut was fine. *Shearwater* now had her two principal sails and we could set off. Two of our oldest sailing friends were visiting family in the area and had come along to see us off. They came aboard for a glass of champagne, admired the improvements and together we all walked to the pub overlooking the marina for a final meal. In my mind I planned to celebrate in the same restaurant on our return. The big unknown was what lay in between. Jan slept on board and approved the re-fit, not least of all the white toilet seat.

Tuesday 7th May
Inshore waters forecast from Land's End to St David's Head
including the Bristol Channel
Wind east or southeast Force 3 or 4, veering south 5 to 7 later.

I called up the marina and requested to lock out at 09.00. I walked up to the car with Jan carrying her bag. She hugged me tightly. I could have been setting off around the world, but had opted for Cardiff, a mere twenty-mile hop across the Severn Estuary. The sun shone brightly as the lights controlling the lock turned green and we slipped our lines. The water roared out of the lock and we descended sedately to sea level. The gates swung slowly open, like the curtains on the first night of a new stage production, and we motored out of the marina. The send-off party stood on the foreshore waving and then they turned and that was it—we were on our way.

Portishead stands at the mouth of the River Avon where it joins the River Severn, the longest river in Great Britain. The shoreline is of thick, glutinous mud which the fast flowing river is constantly rinsing away into thick brown soup. Angling boats regularly fish the waters, although it's a wonder that the fish can ever see the bait, or indeed survive at all. The tidal range is almost 15 metres, one of the largest in the world. For this vast body of water to rise and fall every twelve hours it has to flow extremely quickly. When we set sail the ebb had commenced, and once clear of the long arm of the breakwater the dredged channel was only 50 metres away, and it was a bit like jumping onto a fast travelator. The wind was politely restrained, but we set both sails and ghosted into the swirling current, where the strength of the tide tilted the huge navigation buoys like flimsy reeds. We made only a couple of knots through the water but were bundled along the coast at six knots.

The new chart plotter was showing our position well enough, but the gadget I'd fitted to relay our position on the charts installed on my iPad stubbornly refused to co-operate. The gizmo I'd bought at the Boat Show was designed to create a wireless hot-spot in the boat, which my iPad could connect with. In harbour our position had shone up clearly but it didn't like being out of sight of land. I already had a problem to solve when we arrived in Cardiff.

It is customary, as a token of respect, for a foreign vessel to fly the national flag of another country when entering its waters. This practice has increased in popularity to the point where yachts will even fly the county flag of somewhere like Devon on sailing into their coastline. I jibbed at buying one for every county en route. I had on board the ensigns for Wales and Scotland and when I judged we were half-way across the estuary I ran the red dragon up to our starboard crosstree.

'This might prevent a broadside of slingshot when we enter Cardiff,' I said. Dave rolled his eyes.

Because the tide was much stronger than the wind we crabbed our way across the estuary, searching out the Monkstone Lighthouse, then Cardiff Spit buoy and finally South Cardiff cardinal mark, our turning point to head up towards the dredged deepwater channel the ships use for accessing Cardiff docks. When we turned northwards and furled the sails the mud banks of Cardiff Grounds were high and dry. It was low water, but the pilot notes assured me we could make the entrance to the lock at all states of the tide.

Dave stared in disbelief as I pointed out a tiny creek leading to the lock gates. When we nosed into the ditch the tide was so low that several of the marker buoys were languishing on their sides in the mud. I called up the barrage lock control and requested permission to enter. They barked back with the number of the lock we were to enter. Five minutes later they called the boat again.

'Make all speed *Shearwater*,' which was their polite way of telling us to stop messing about. The depth sounder showed 0.8 metres under our keels as we crept into the lock basin. I supposed you only needed enough water to float, but it seemed devilishly tight. We made it, and after more taut ropes and gushing water we rose the ten metres or so to emerge into Cardiff Bay. We motored round into Penarth Marina and tied up on a visitors' pontoon. It was 1315 and we'd completed our first passage of the trip. After lunch in the cockpit and a cheeky beer we snoozed in the afternoon sun. This was the life.

We had moored alongside a fishing boat and I asked the skipper, a wizened old boy, the way to the shops. He pointed at a hill which he said the locals refer to as 'Cardiac Incline.' In the late afternoon we flogged up the slope, then along winding streets lined with tall, proud buildings reflecting a former prosperity when the docks were alive with commercial shipping, instead of holiday homes and plastic pleasure boats. Penarth has a pier in the grand Edwardian style. We treated ourselves to ice creams and promenaded to the end where two fishermen were casting long beach rods out into the sea. One of them had a big radio blasting out the sixties hit *Telstar*. It felt as though we'd sailed through a time warp.

The rest of that week proved to be a mixture of relaxation and frustration. As forecast, the wind blew strongly from the west, interspersed with heavy showers. The first day, Wednesday, was easily occupied. Dave had forgotten his fleece jacket so we strolled to the local chandlers where he made his first purchase of the trip and I bought some metal brackets to stiffen up the cockpit locker shelving, now groaning under the strain of all the 'must have' kit I'd brought on board. In between the rain showers we busied ourselves doing boat jobs. A telephone call to the chart plotter chaps revealed I needed to upgrade my electronic charts on the iPad. I paid up and downloaded enough electronic charts to guide us around the British Isles, and even Holland if my navigation went badly awry.

In the evening we found a local pub, the large modern sort with good value grub, and a pool table overlooked by an oversized TV screen displaying round the clock sport. Office workers and business suits were sitting on high bar stools being chatted up by glamorous women. There was a corner to suit everyone. The locals were occupying the pool table, wearing tight tee shirts which struggled to contain bulging muscles. Their bare arms were adorned with wondrous tattoos, and the only conversation, in short, heavily-accented bursts, focused on the next anatomical art work. After observing play for a few matches we summoned up the courage to slap our coins on the edge of the table. 'My money's on the one with the check shirt,' was the closest they got to introducing themselves. Perhaps we didn't try too hard either. It was my first encounter with the natives. Would I end up conducting a survey of pool tables and players around the coast, or perhaps a regional comparison of tattoos? He was right. I was the 'checked shirt one' and the victor. We left the table to the locals and escaped back to the boat.

As the week wore on the weather remained stubbornly unhelpful. If we'd been touring in a camper van the odd shower and a fresh breeze would hardly have been reason to stay put in the camp site, but we were still feeling our sea legs with a newly rigged boat. There might be a time later in the voyage when I'd have to pit myself against the elements. For the moment we could afford to wait for the right conditions. In addition to the rain it grew cold. Our ice creams and stroll on the pier now seemed a distant memory.

One of the small luxuries on *Shearwater* is a diesel heater. Just press the button and the fan wafts warm air into the cabin. It worked perfectly during the Siberian re-fit but in Penarth decided to shut itself down after a few minutes' operation. The engineers in the marina were advertising the same make of heater so it seemed a convenient place to get it fixed. This prompted a visit to the boat by the yard manager, complete with clipboard and order form. I could see it was not going to end well.

After much wailing and gnashing of teeth, not least from Dave and me as we contorted ourselves head first in the rear locker to remove the unit, the engineer pronounced my kit 'obsolete' and said he would have to send it away 'to see if they can fix it.' I handed over a king's ransom on account and they promised to forward it to me at Holyhead, on the optimistic assumption that I would eventually get that far at least.

The days ticked by and high winds, driving rain, thunder and lightning all inflicted themselves on *Shearwater* and her crew. One evening we even resorted to cooking on board and settling down to watch a film that I had downloaded on my iPad. I could have been doing this at home, I sulked. The plan had been to pick up our next crew, Chris, in Fishguard, on Sunday. Each day that passed necessitated a re-think and finally on Saturday I phoned him to say that we planned to break out the following day and head towards Swansea. The passage was about forty miles but I reckoned that with the benefit of the powerful ebb we could do it in less than six hours. Less would be good because the weather on Sunday was not forecast to be much better than any other day.

Sunday 12th May
Inshore Forecast
Wind west increasing Force 5 or 6 occasionally.
Sea moderate, occasionally rough.
Rain, then drizzle. Visibility moderate or poor.

If it hadn't been for my promise to Chris and the fear of getting stuck in Penarth forever, I would have rolled over and gone back to sleep. We ate some porridge, and cast off towards Swansea. At least it wasn't raining as we emerged from the barrage lock and motored out to Lavernock Point where we joined the rush of the ebb tide sweeping westwards. We set the mainsail with two reefs and reefed the genoa. *Shearwater* raced along, sailing with all the vitality of a dog just let off the lead. Even her reluctant crew were enjoying the sail, glad to be moving on at last. The rain arrived to test our resolve, and our foul weather clothing. The visibility reduced to a wet misty gloom, through which we could occasionally glimpse the shore. Breaksea Point, the southernmost point on the Welsh coastline, came and went. Dave was checking our progress on his hand-held plotter, a steam driven version resembling the house-brick sized mobile phones in old films. He confirmed the new plotter to be correct, and a bright triangle on the new iPad charts showed a position which matched the others. Well, we're all agreed on that, I thought.

Then I noticed the chart plotter was failing to display another of its magical tricks, the AIS. In recent years an enormous advancement in navigational safety has been the development of the Automatic Identification Signal (AIS). The position, course and speed of vessels, their name and radio call sign, are automatically transmitted at regular intervals and can be plotted on electronic charts. All medium to large ships are obliged to fit transmitters and anyone with the receiving kit can monitor them. For small yachts it's more effective than radar because, armed with a ship's name and call sign, you can call it up directly to announce your presence. My plotter is a 'combo,' neatly including this device and the basic navigational aid in one unit. Only it wasn't working. I sighed; another thing to sort out in harbour. I just hoped there were no big ships heading our way in the mist.

The waves were large but not dangerous and *Shearwater* made good progress. Two navigational dangers, the Nash Sand and the Scar, obstructed our approach to Swansea Bay. They are well marked by buoys appropriately called East Nash, South Nash and West Nash. 'Don't make a hash of the Nash' went through my mind. As for the Scar, I shuddered to think how it got its name. The rain and breaking seas made it difficult to spot Mumbles Lighthouse which was somewhere on the western corner of Swansea Bay, so we had to entrust our safety to the plotter. When I judged our position to be good, we changed course to bear away towards the south cardinal buoy marking the entrance to the dredged channel leading into Swansea Harbour. It was low water. I knew the sandbanks of Swansea Bay would be uncovered and could hear the breaking waves, but see nothing. I called the Swansea coastguard on the radio.

'Do you have any information on the state of the sea in the approaches to the harbour?' I asked.

'Yacht *Shearwater*, we're situated at Mumbles Head. We've got 25 knots of wind here, but I can't tell you anything about the harbour entrance. You'll have to make your own judgment.'

I peered ahead into the gloom. It's unnerving when you're sailing downwind towards an unknown entrance in poor visibility. On the one hand you are eager to get into the harbour and out of the weather, but also anxious not to wrap the boat up on the final approach. The outer cardinal buoy loomed into view. The channel is supposed to be dredged to a minimum depth of four metres but the note on the charts read, 'the depths change frequently due to shifting sands.' That's handy, I thought. We rounded up into the wind and dropped the sails. The tide still covered the sandbanks marking the edges of the channel and obscured their exact position, so we chugged slowly along, carefully following a compass course to pick up the harbour entrance. My eyes were glued to the depth sounder. I could feel my pulse quicken.

We were no more than a couple of hundred metres (or a cable, as we sailors say) from the harbour breakwater when we first saw it. Sandbanks encircled the entrance with waves smashing irritably against the high concrete arms. The gap between the breakwaters was wide and the position of the safe channel now obvious. I breathed a sigh of relief. Once through, in the lee of the breakwater arms, the wind eased but the drizzle fell vertically down our necks. We motored slowly into the harbour amongst the drab, rain-doused structures. It was too early for the lock into Swansea marina so we picked up a holding buoy downstream from the barrage, clear of the weir over which the River Tawe roared. It was good to get into the cabin and brew a cup of tea. Before long the watch keeper called me on the radio to say he was filling the lock and as we approached the gates I spotted a familiar profile standing on the pontoon in full sailing gear. He took our lines.

'Nice weather, Chris,' I shouted. 'Welcome to the voyage.'

We were allocated a berth at one end of the marina under the tall gaze of the apartment blocks which now form the Maritime Quarter. We made fast, stripped off our dripping gear and put the washboards in. After formal introductions I made supper and we yarned about the week before and plans for the week ahead. That was it for the night.

I had established a routine of setting the alarm for seven each morning. By that time the Met Office had posted the inshore waters forecast on the internet. The news was discouraging. 'Strong westerly winds, moderate to high seas, rain and poor visibility.' No locusts at least, I mused, and rolled back to sleep.

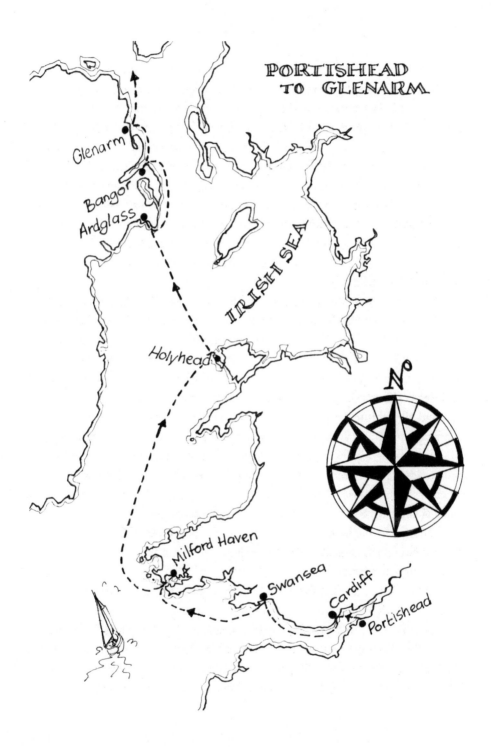

We hadn't made much progress in the first week and already the prospects were not looking good for week two. I was developing a depressing fear that the weather would dash my plans at the very outset, and resolved that the only way to approach the trip was to consider it as a three months cruise to wherever I could make it. If I completed the circumnavigation it would be a bonus. Neither Chris nor Dave seemed particularly keen to rise; they could hear the rain lashing the deck. When I did stir to put the kettle on the downpour had eased and a blustery wind rocked the boats in the marina. Like Penarth, the marina has been created in a former dock, now surrounded with tall red brick apartment blocks, designed to emulate the warehouses which once lined the quays. Chris, the architect, gave it top marks but we all agreed the sky-blue paintwork on the balconies and steelwork was already looking dated.

Over breakfast we discussed our plans for the week. Chris had a rail ticket home booked from Holyhead for Saturday, Dave was on board for another fortnight and I had the rest of the UK to get round. We all agreed the next passage of fifty miles to Milford Haven required better weather than was forecast. We abandoned any plans to sail that day and set off to stroll around the bay to Mumbles Head. The sun was warm but a piercing, cold wind prompted the wearing of hats and gloves. It felt more like October than spring. The beach was deserted, apart from the odd stalwart dog walker, but by the time we had tramped around the long curving bay more people had trickled out to brave the elements. The promenade was scattered with the remains of the railway which once connected Mumbles with Swansea. Built in 1804, it became the world's first and longest running fare-paying passenger railway. It finally closed in 1960, having been propelled during its life by horse, sail, steam, diesel, petrol and electricity. Thank heavens its opening coincided with the abolition of slavery. They might have been tempted to go for the full set.

Nowadays, Mumbles is famous for the lighthouse which presides over the rocks on the edge of the bay. This morning the rocks were under siege from an ugly pounding sea; there were no regrets at abandoning the sailing. When we arrived the pier was closed for refurbishment. We had some lunch and caught the bus back into Swansea, climbing aboard *Shearwater* as the heavens opened. That evening we ate in the Italian restaurant overlooking the marina and that was another day gone. The next morning we all got up early assuming we would be setting sail. The wind had eased but heavy rain was forecast. The day after promised better, but only after a slow moving trough passed through. Reluctantly we decided to postpone our departure yet again. As the tour leader I felt obliged to put on some entertainment. I discovered a museum on the harbour front and we whiled away an interesting few hours understanding Swansea's redevelopment following the demise of the steel and coal industry. It had been a hard act to follow. At its height all the steam-powered ships of the Royal Navy specified coal mined in South Wales, loaded at Swansea. All the usual heavy industries were supported but in common with many similar cities, by the mid-forties these had fallen into decline. The city managed to attract significant investment, much of it led by Government—the Driver and Vehicle Licensing Centre alone employing more than 5,000 people.

At lunchtime it was a toss-up between visiting the Dylan Thomas Centre and supping a pint in one of the historic old pubs near the harbour. We decided there was only so much knowledge one could absorb on a wet day, so the pub won. The afternoon wasn't a complete write off because, after lunch, Dave purchased some LED adhesive strip lighting for his proposed improvements to the galley area. I bought some wood for a pelmet to house the lighting and Chris directed the design and construction. This kept us busy until dinner time. We ate on board, admiring the low key lighting that now washed over the stove and sink.

A few boating niggles remained. We were getting water in the bilge, and with a relatively flat bottomed hull *Shearwater* has only to heel in the breeze (which she had done for nearly the entire beat down from Cardiff) for most of the wet stuff to wash into the base lockers. A dab of the finger, cautiously licked, tasted salty. I bought a stirrup pump to extract the last drop from every nook and cranny and eyed the keel bolts suspiciously. These are the heavy bolts which attach the twin keels to the hull. They are inclined to weep in older boats and I hoped they weren't the source of our water.

Wednesday morning dawned with yet another disappointing forecast. The trough had passed through but a strong wind warning was in force, suggesting winds in excess of Force 5, from the west. I moaned to the guy in the yacht chandlers.

'When the wind's hard from the west no one gets out of the Bristol Channel,' he said. 'They all try, and come unstuck at the Mumbles. It should be better tomorrow.'

Back on the boat I thought about what he'd said. I was beginning to regret my choice of starting place. Other circumnavigation accounts I had read missed out the Bristol Channel altogether, hopping straight across from Padstow to Milford Haven. I realised that to make any decent progress you have to take the ebb tide flowing west. With any strength of wind from that direction the seas immediately kick up, making life unpleasant for little yachts. Still, it was a bit late to be wishing to have started somewhere else.

We spent the day inspecting the floating museum exhibits in the harbour. There was an old steam-powered light ship, and a beautifully restored pilot cutter. The regulations governing their operation required three pilots to attend any ship and compete for the work. No wonder they needed fast ships to race out to meet incoming vessels. Some of them took to sheltering in the Scillies to get a jump on the competition. The workmanship on them was beautiful and it was encouraging to see a local authority had taken the initiative to ensure their preservation.

At tea time our spirits rose. The evening forecast for the next twenty four hours promised north easterly winds Force 2 to 3, occasionally 4. The skies cleared and we had a treat that evening, taking the lift to the 28th floor of the magnificent Meridian Tower. We sat in the bar enjoying the sensational views over Swansea Bay and the Maritime Quarter. We were tempted to stay and eat but it looked appropriately pricey, so we opted for the Indian restaurant in the harbour. We walked back to the boat exuding the warmth of a good curry and perhaps the prospect of finally setting sail the next day. No one said anything when it began to rain.

At last, on Thursday, we were able to resume the voyage. It was fifty one miles to Milford Haven, and if all went to plan we planned to arrive at 1900hrs. It was a pleasant day, and a gentle breeze pushed us along nicely. At last the muddy waters of the Severn estuary gave way to clear blue sea. I was greatly relieved to be under way again and to feel the warmth of the sun on my back. The cliffs of the Gower peninsular slipped by and we began our crossing of Carmarthen Bay. I noticed on the chart that most of the bay was marked with red flame-shaped icons indicating a military firing practice area. I thought it prudent to call the Coastguard who gave me details of the live firing taking place that day and advised me to contact the range control on channel 73. No sooner had I ended the call when the radio piped up.

'Yacht *Shearwater*, this is Manorbier range control. Please give your current position. Over.'

I glanced at the chart plotter and responded. There was a moment's silence then his voice again, 'Yacht *Shearwater*, you are in the middle of a live firing range. You should immediately alter course to steer 180° for five miles. Over'

My heart missed a beat. I shouted up to Chris who put the helm over. The wind was dying so we started the engine. After a few minutes the range control came back to query my position. I realised I'd misread the plotter. They knew exactly where we were from their radar, and probably knew the colour of my underpants.

'*Shearwater*, you are not in a live firing range area but soon will be. We suggest you alter course for Caldey Island and await further instructions.'

I thought about our options. There is no prohibition on sailing through a range but something about his tone of voice suggested they wouldn't want to hang about whilst we bumbled through the area at five knots. I confirmed our agreement and we altered course again. During the next two hours we pottered about listening to the comings and goings on the radio. This was no ordinary pop gun range. It transpired that Manorbier is the only range in the UK where they fire high-velocity anti-aircraft missiles. Just our luck. Eventually we were told we could resume our passage and they thanked us for our co-operation. Not much choice, but still.

By now the wind had died away completely and the tide was starting to turn against us. We made slow progress towards St Govans Head. I became more interested in small red flames on the chart. According to the notes in Reeds almanac, the Castlemartin range finished operations at 1800. I called them up for confirmation.

'Yacht *Shearwater*, yes we do finish firing operations at 1800. But we then commence again at 1930.' Clearly the almanac had overlooked the possibility of evening classes. I sighed and asked what he proposed, knowing the answer.

'I will give you a suggested course to take you safely clear of the range area.' When I plotted it I groaned. We were being taken in a big sweep south around the perimeter. It was 2100 and growing dark before we were finally advised it was safe to resume our course. As we picked up the leading mark for the entrance to Milford Haven the sky behind us lit up with red tracer fire accompanied by thunderous explosions.

'It's not as good as Dartmouth Regatta,' said Chris.

Five

∾

Inshore Forecast for 24 hours from 12.00 17th May 2013
From St David's Head to Great Orme
Wind north or northeast, backing northwest later Force 4 or 5.
Sea slight, rain later. Visibility good, occasionally moderate.

MILFORD HAVEN COMBINES A BEAUTIFUL natural harbour with ac-commodating the fourth largest commercial shipping tonnage in the UK. An enormous oil terminal has been built next to one of the biggest liquid gas ter-minals in the world. Every few hours a vast tanker creeps up the Sound to unload the gas for cooking the Sunday roast. This has resulted in a crowded waterway, bristling with flashing beacons and buoys and a harbour resembling a film set from Star Wars. Wearily we edged up the eastern channel, ticking off the buoys and generally keeping out of the way. Had we arrived in daylight we could have an-chored in one of the pleasant little bays the pilot outlined. But we were tired and disgruntled and wanted a good night's sleep, so we motored the extra mile up the estuary to lock into Milford Haven Marina. The lock gates were open when we tied up, but the lock keeper cheerfully reported the next lock wouldn't operate for another hour. It was a cold, crisp evening and we skulked in the cabin drinking coffee laced with a stiff tot, and didn't finally moor up until 0130. The log showed we'd covered another 26 miles as our part in supporting the armed forces. Revel-ling in that satisfaction we collapsed into bed.

When I awoke I could see my breath in the sunlight leaching through the fore hatch. I warmed some clothes in my sleeping bag and flicked the phone for the inshore forecast.

Over breakfast we discussed the options. I fancied a day in Milford Haven. Chris was keen to get to Holyhead, although the chances of him catching his train home seemed remote. Dave was relaxed either way. A passage direct to Holyhead would put us back on schedule. It seemed a shame to be leaving so soon but I was keen to break out of the Bristol Channel and the forecast seemed half decent. We would be sailing 120 miles out past Skomer Island, then across St Bride's Bay to round the Bishops and Clerks, an outcrop of ugly rocks guarding St David's Head. After steering due north across Cardigan Bay to pick up the lighthouse on Bardsey Island, we would bear away up the Lleyn Peninsula and then on to Holyhead. The pilot book was full of dire warnings about each of the headlands, the rip tides, overfalls and busy shipping lanes. There wasn't much on sea serpents. Perhaps these were omitted to provide a little surprise on the way. The passage would mean spending a night at sea and missing out Fishguard, Pwllhelli, and a visit to an old pal who lives at Aberdovey. But the overall weather pattern gave us a shot at getting back on schedule and I needed a boost to my flagging spirits.

We decided to go for it and resolved to set off at 1100. First we had to provision up and re-fuel. I literally trotted along to the supermarket as I was keen to depart during the period of free flow in the lock. This is when the tide is high enough to keep the lock gates open. We'd seen the night before how long it took to 'fill the bath.' I grabbed some ready meals and stocked up on chocolate snacks. The treat box was quickly becoming a much loved part of the boat. Chocolate biscuits and all manner of bad-for-you tasties were stored in a box to be consumed without guilt when the going got rough, or come to think about it even in a flat calm.

On the way back I went to pay our marina dues and recounted our tale of military misery the day before. The marina hand told me about an exchange he'd heard over the VHF between a tanker captain and one of the range control officers, which went something like this:

'Captain, we'd like you to alter course to steer 270°.'

'But if I do that I'll miss the tide for getting to our berth in the refinery.'

'Captain, you are steaming into a live firing range. I must advise you to alter course.'

'Are you going to explain to my owner why the cargo was delayed?'

'Would you rather explain to your owner how his ship came to be blown out of the water?'

A pause.

'Range control, we are altering course to 270°.'

We cleared the harbour at 1100 and motored down the estuary on a crisp spring morning. I felt a pang of regret as we steamed past Sandy Haven Bay, The Dales and the other anchorages I'd savoured in my winter planning. Another time, I sighed. I knew I couldn't afford to get too far behind this early on in the trip. *Shearwater* danced across the sparkling sea, close hauled under Dave's spirited helming. We half-raced a couple of yachts who peeled away to anchor in the lee of Skomer. Sea birds screamed in delight as they glided back and forth in the blustery breeze. As we cleared the island, the wind freshened. *Shearwater* heeled hard over to the point where the steering became heavy. Chris sagely observed she would sail more easily with a reef in the mainsail. He was right of course, so we shortened sail. We lost no boat speed but the motion was easier and the contents of the cabin shelves abandoned their acrobatic display.

We remained on starboard tack for a few hours heading out into St George's Channel towards Ireland. I'd planned the time of our departure so the flood tide would sweep us northwards and clear of the treacherous Bishops. I set a waypoint in the chart plotter for Bardsey Island, 58 miles away. Waypoints are to sailors what cairns are to hill walkers. The only difference is you place them where you want. On an electronic chart it's easy—you just position the cursor and press the button. Up pops the course direction and distance off, or DTW. This is great if the wind or tide permit you to aim for the chosen waypoint. It's almost a case of following the dotted line. But when the wind is blowing from that direction you have to tack or beat towards your destination, zig-zagging up the course, so to speak.

The tide in St George's Channel runs strongly. After a few hours it turned against us and although *Shearwater* was resolutely sailing onwards we were being carried backwards. On a long passage, at the end of each hour I always enter our current position in the deck log and note the DTW, in this case for Bardsey Island, North Wales. It was discouraging to note that in two hours we had only made good five miles towards our waypoint. When you are beating, even the sleekest racing yacht can only sail to within thirty degrees of the point the wind is blowing from. With a heavy, bilge keel cruising boat, this angle reduces to forty degrees. Then if you add on some leeway and a foul tide, it doesn't take Einstein to work out you could be gaily sailing back and forth all day and get nowhere. It could be worse, I told the crew, recounting the tales of the square riggers. Setting out from Belfast for Australia they sometimes found it so difficult tacking down the Irish Sea, they turned tail and sailed back around the Northern tip of Ireland in order to make longer tacks out into the Atlantic. We agreed this was a bit extreme, so I started the engine.

By mid afternoon our position was such that it would have been more convenient to head for the coast of Southern Ireland. I resisted the temptation (if only because Chris had his rail ticket). The wind backed slightly and I calculated we could alter course and make Bardsey Island, hoping the wind would shift further round during the night and improve our sailing angle still further. We tacked onto port and we settled down for the night passage. After woofing down a couple of ready meals, which improved morale, we agreed on a watch system. With three crew we could afford to have one on the helm who would go off watch at the end of his trick, one on half watch dozing in the cockpit or making a hot drink and keeping the helm company, and one in his bunk. We decided on one hour tricks, so you could be sleeping for one hour in every three. Chris embraced this with enthusiasm. At the end of his spell on the helm he was down in the cabin and tucked up in his sleeping bag in a trice. Getting him back up in the cockpit took a bit longer.

Out in the centre of the channel a deep swell tossed *Shearwater* like a cat with a toy. Every normally flat surface sprang into life threatening to tip the unwary on his back, or worse, over the side. The old adage 'one hand for the boat and one for yourself' says it all. We all wore harnesses and lanyards clipped on to anchorage points. Moving round the cockpit can result in tangles and snags enough to appreciate the frustration of dogs on leads encountering lampposts.

It was a pleasant evening, the sun staying with us until it slipped down below the horizon, leaving a chill that gnawed at our clothing. Soon enough we were engulfed in darkness, our own tiny world, whose boundaries were the reflections of the navigation lights on the forward guard rail and the warm glowing lights from the instrument panel above the companion way. We started the watch system, rotating through our duties. The helm, whilst primarily ensuring the boat stays on course, is the main look out, every few minutes peering ahead and behind the boat to pick up the lights of other vessels. Above us the clouds were broken, stars flickering in the night sky in between. You don't always know how good the visibility is until you see another object. What appears to be a clear path ahead could be a cloud bank concealing a ship. I cursed the fault on the chart plotter, which should have been showing us all the large vessels in the area. The AIS report remained stubbornly blank.

Around midnight I came off the helm. In eleven hours we had made good only 28 miles. Chris took an age to get his gear on, and by the time I'd entered our position in the log, removed my gear and crawled into bed my precious hour's sleep had dwindled. All too quickly I was up again making a drink. Perhaps we should have gone for longer spells, giving more sleep but longer on the helm. I'd made plenty of night passages over the years and only a few stuck out as pleasurable, invariably in warmer seas with dark black, star-studded skies to wonder at. This sort of passage was one to endure, the price to reach a distant destination and in our case to recover days wasted stormbound. At least *Shearwater* was performing well under her new rig, determinedly ploughing up the Irish Sea.

Slowly the DTW reduced, and by first light the tide turned in our favour and we were making good progress. It's always a relief to greet the dawn light. A period of dull gloom grows steadily and you search for the sun to warm damp, chilled bones. The coastline of North Wales appeared as a thin smear on the horizon. The wind had backed to north-north-west, better than before but not the forecast south-west. I was able to adjust our course, to stand well off Bardsey Island and head straight for South Stack. For the first time, with reasonable confidence, I could estimate our time of arrival to be early afternoon. With sunrise the wind died away and the engine took an increasing responsibility for our progress.

The charted overfalls off South Stack materialised and I was glad our course took us well clear. Spiteful breaking waves, or white horses, roamed up and down, threatening retribution on any vessels having the temerity to face them down. It's a big moment on a long passage when you have been on the same tack for several hours and then, at last, you reach a turning point, a waypoint, a buoy or landmark where you can significantly alter course. With the light house off our stern quarter I eased the helm for the run down towards the breakwaters of Holyhead harbour.

We'd kept the watch system operating during the morning, not least because we were all tired. Normally the anticipation of arriving at a new destination terminates the routine, with all the crew keen to espy new land. Dave and I were amused to see Chris hot-foot it to his bunk when we seemed barely an hour from arrival. We pulled his leg and it transpired he had been popping sea sickness tablets, which tend to induce drowsiness. He struggled back on deck to fasten the fenders, and we berthed in the marina. Chris had missed his train but give or take an hour or so we were back on schedule.

I was expecting to feel elated, but Holyhead Harbour presented a dispiriting sight. The leaden sky made the long stone harbour breakwater appear even more drab. A fleet of squib keelboats were racing in the harbour, but even their bright red sails failed to lift the surroundings. In the distance we could just make out the cliffs of North Stack. After the sunshine we'd left in Milford Haven it really felt like the bleak north. I hoped that Scotland would be more colourful. The water in the harbour was crystal clear, revealing the yellow crustaceans clinging to the pontoon floats. Beneath the surface I could see the whole of *Shearwater*'s hull and both keels, which was reassuring.

Dave went off to recce the showers. Chris got the shore power hooked up and I unstowed the fan heater. I hoped that with a bit of luck the diesel heater would have arrived from Penarth, all repaired. Dave came back looking suitably clean. 'They asked if I was the skipper,' he said. 'I told them you'd be up shortly to fill in the paperwork.'

Chris and I wandered up to the marina reception. On our return Dave had brewed some tea.

'Good showers, lads?' he asked.

'Very posh,' Chris replied. 'I've never had a private cubicle before.'

'How d'yer mean?' asked Dave.

'They gave me a key to a private shower cubicle, with its own loo and basin; everything.'

Dave looked at me. 'Did you get one of those?'

'Yes, it was great. Just had to sign for the key.'

Dave looked crestfallen. 'They didn't offer me one of those' he whispered. 'I was directed down the corridor to a communal changing room. I had a hell of a job to get any warm water.'

Chris and I grinned at each other.

'Must have been for 'other ranks'' I said.

The history of Holyhead Sailing Club stretches back to 1905. The clubhouse overlooks the harbour and serves good beer. We sat in the lounge, studying the faded photos of past club heroes and winners, contentedly waiting for the restaurant to open. Mala, who gave the place her name, did us proud and full of food and beer we tottered back to *Shearwater* and slept soundly.

The next morning, Sunday, was a crew changeover day. Chris pecked away at his mobile phone and bought a rail ticket home. Dave and I waved him off and began some boat jobs. On lifting the bottom boards I was dismayed to see again the bilges full of water. I'd specifically mopped them dry in Swansea. I looked hard at the row of keel bolts which secure the keels to the hull; there were no telltale rusty streaks to suggest they were the culprit. I went forward and unbolted the hatch to the chain locker. We'd been 'shipping it green' on our way up the Irish Sea—I supposed the water could have washed in via the hawse-pipe through which the anchor chain ran out over the newly installed anchor winch.

Dave played a hose over the winch and straight away I could see the problem. My torch beam lit up a steady stream dripping into the chain locker, which in turn drained down into the bilge. Removing the outer casing of the winch revealed gaping holes under the edge of the assembly through which quantities of the St George's Channel had been entering the boat unannounced. Half a tube of sealant later we had ourselves a water-tight boat.

The next issue was the pathetic reception on the FM radio. I'd fitted a new radio during the re-fit. Dave was convinced I'd sabotaged the Radio 4 signal to deny him his daily fix of *The Archers*. I might have done had I known how. After mulling over the possible reasons we re-connected the aerial using the remains of the old VHF antenna lead. I stripped back the outer sheath and connected this to the jack plug. I fumbled around at the back of the radio and turned it on. Nothing.

'Let me look,' said Dave. He fiddled about for a minute. There was a crackle and then the clichéd melody of country dance music sang out loud and clear. He turned to me and frowned. 'You put the jack plug into the wrong socket. Was that your attempt to sabotage my programme?' I held up my hands. The radio was fine from then on.

It wasn't a bad morning. I'd downgraded my expectations of the weather. No rain was good, weak sunshine very acceptable. Peter, our new crew, sent a text to say he was on the train and would arrive after lunch. Having solved two boat problems we ambled off along the waterfront, watching the boats racing in the harbour. A large cruise ship had docked by the ferry terminal and we met groups of German passengers taking the air. My German isn't very good but I couldn't help feeling the main thrust of the conversation was along the lines of 'What the hell have they brought us here for?'

Peter arrived and stowed his gear. I outlined the sailing plans for the week ahead. Weather permitting we would sail to the Isle of Man, and then head for the Northern Irish coast and make our way up to Bangor, in Belfast Lough, from where we would all jump on a plane home and I'd spend a week with Jan. The only fly in the ointment was the weather. A deep low-pressure system was heading in from the Atlantic. That evening we made the cabin snug and ate on board, and turned in hoping for a change of fortune the next day.

The dice rolled against us and Monday morning dawned wet and windy. The seas surged in and smashed against the outer harbour walls, throwing clouds of spray over the top. When the rain eased we walked up into the town. It was more depressing than the weather. The main shopping street was half boarded up and the shops that were still trading wore a shroud of disinterest and resignation. I was looking for a battery charger for my camera. I entered one of those 'sell everything' establishments and made my enquiry. The guy behind the counter hardly looked up. 'No, mate nothing like that. You won't get one here. You won't get anything here.'

I dared to ask what the problem was.

'Since the aluminium plant closed there's nothing left. This place is finished.'

We resisted the implied invitation to step outside and slit our throats and trudged back to the marina. Waiting in the office was a parcel from Swansea, containing the diesel heater. It worked after a fashion but still kept on cutting out just when the cabin was getting nice and snug. With a bit of luck the weather would improve soon and we wouldn't need it. We packed away the tools and walked up to the marina reception. I wasn't with Dave when he went for his shower but later, when we compared notes, it became apparent that once again he'd not been offered a private cubicle. Pete enjoyed the joke as well.

Mala's was closed so we found a pub apparently offering very average bar food and were not deceived. We felt a walk might aid digestion of the stodgy load. We meandered along the country lanes, past abandoned hotels, wondering what they might have looked like in their glory days. Even the boatyard seemed forlorn, with more boats looking forgotten than being prepared for a new season. We took another almost fatalistic glance at the weather forecast in the marina reception, and back on board *Shearwater* held a council of war. The weather pattern looked bad and established for the next few days. There was a risk that even if we made it to the Isle of Man we might get stuck there and our retreat home would be difficult. Sadly we decided to abort the week's trip and take the train home the next day. Peter had made the long journey and lost a week's work all for nothing. I decided to bring forward my home break and return with new crew when the weather settled down. It was very frustrating but at least I had a week in hand and in the overall scheme of things was not yet seriously behind schedule.

We were up and busy the next morning. Dave felt the rig needed tightening. After our antics off the Devon coast the autumn before he held a particular interest in this part of the boat. We took a turn in each of the bottle screws that tension the shrouds. I unwired the chart plotter which was posted back to the manufacturers to repair the non functioning AIS. The ship's clock, a brass chronometer, was having a tantrum. When we arrived in Holyhead it appeared to have gone slow. I changed the battery and re-set the time but an hour later it was showing a completely different time. I tapped the glass, a bit like one would with a barometer, and the minute hand dropped vertical. Step in Dave, the engineer who took the back off.

'Someone's been in here before,' he proclaimed before re-securing the hand.

We checked all the mooring lines and fenders and left *Shearwater* in the care of the marina staff. In the taxi to the station we asked the driver what had gone wrong with the town. 'What about the ferries?' I asked. 'Don't they bring in some trade?' He replied that the ferries were all crewed by Eastern Europeans who worked a two week shift, never left the ship and during their leave shot off home with their earnings. I thought about Swansea.

'They need a big government office here,' I said.

Three hours and a couple of trains later I was back in the arms of my wife, who surveyed my newly sprouted beard with amusement.

'Shouldn't it be growing straight?' she asked. I stared in the bathroom mirror. She had a point. It was sticking out all over my chin. After a couple of days of scratching the itch the razor blade got to work. I rubbed my smooth chops with a sigh of satisfaction.

Six

⁊

WHEN PLANNING THE TRIP I included in the schedule a couple of
weeks' rest. I'd imagined, that after the intense concentration on passage
planning, provisioning and sailing the boat, relaxing at home would be bliss. It
didn't work out that way. No sooner had I caught up with the village gossip and
walked the garden a couple of times than I found myself studying the shipping
forecasts to see what I was missing. The big blow which had curtailed our plans
was followed by settled weather, and moderate south-westerly winds that would
have been ideal for the passage across to the Isle of Man. Frustratingly, I was in
Derbyshire without a crew.

No one was available at short notice but Simon and Joy, who originally
planned to meet the boat in Bangor, offered to join up early and sail with me to
Northern Ireland where we would pick up the last crew member, Colin. With this
plan in place I could relax and before I knew it I was on the train back to Holyhead. *Shearwater* was resting quietly in her berth, but the weather was starting to
deteriorate and a fresh breeze sprayed fine rain over the harbour wall. I re-fitted
the chart plotter, and was greatly relieved to see it working as intended. We now
had AIS.

Later in the afternoon Simon and Joy arrived, courtesy of a lift from some
other Ogston sailors. Over dinner in Mala's we discussed possible plans. I'd studied the pilot for the Isle of Man. We would only have time to stop overnight, so I
ruled out Douglas and Peel because both would add distance to the passage. That
left Port St Mary on the southern tip.

This was to be the first week of my voyage with a relatively unknown crew.
Simon and Joy are keen dinghy sailors but they had little experience of sailing
offshore. Early on Joy had confided that she was worried about sea sickness. I
tried to reassure her that it was very common, probably wouldn't affect her and
didn't cause me any concern. Nevertheless, I knew the next section across open

sea would take at least twelve hours and I was keen to play down the demands of the passage. I said although the wind was forecast to ease later in the week the seas would remain lumpy and suggested it might be better to spend a day settling in before we set sail. The next morning the wind was still growling over the harbour walls but the sun was breaking through and we decided to hike over the cliffs to South Stack lighthouse. We set off along a disused railway track, now converted to a nature trail, and then climbed the winding cliff top path to the bird sanctuary overlooking South Stack and the magnificent whitewashed lighthouse. We drank coffee in the little café staring down at the angry sea, churned up in the overfalls running past the headland. I knew it had been the right decision to delay our departure.

The walk was a good opportunity to get to know each other. Simon and Joy sail together regularly and have a great rapport, endlessly ragging each other. Simon once served in the armed forces, and only a couple of years earlier he'd suffered a life threatening brain aneurism. He's a walking miracle, as statistically only one in nine people survives his illness and of those only one in nine escapes serious brain injury. Joy quipped that he could only consider himself part of the first category. He gets bad headaches, and when he's feeling good is inclined to be hyperactive. Joy told me about her previous career as a police officer, before completing a business degree. Despite her misgivings about sea sickness, I had her down as a tough cookie. Hopefully we wouldn't need any of their former skills but we were heading for Northern Ireland so who knows, I thought.

Back from our walk we found the wind buffeting *Shearwater* in her berth. After lunch I suggested we took the boat to re-fuel so as to be ready for an early departure the next morning. The manoeuvre gave me a chance to observe boat handling skills. We practiced berthing amongst the half full pontoons. We had a few antics, slipping knots and some knitting but no one fell in and *Shearwater* was made fast without too much shouting and without any bruises or insurance claims.

In the evening we ate on board and studied the latest weather forecast. Although reducing in strength the wind had reverted to the north which, surprise, surprise, was the direction of our proposed course to the Isle of Man. After the marathon beat up the Irish Sea I was keen to avoid another long slog to windward and reluctantly elected to abandon our visit to the island. It was a shame because I'd never been there and hoped to meet up with another Ogston sailor who was watching the TT motor cycle racing.

With the wind in the north I said we could hold a course northwest and make the Northern Irish coast somewhere around Strangford Lough. I reckoned that if the wind then backed round to the west and blew up we could still work our way up to Bangor, sheltering in the lee of the land. We had a plan, and barring any dramatic changes in the weather, would depart the next day. For the second time on the cruise I'd be ignoring superstition and setting sail on a Friday. I couldn't afford to have every Friday off.

Shipping Forecast for 24 hours from 06.00 Friday 1st June
Irish Sea
Wind northwest Force 3 or 4 increasing 4 or 5 for a time.
Sea slight or moderate.

I was up at seven to check the forecast and make porridge. Typically, the weather gods had rumbled our plans and the wind was now forecast to blow from the northwest, not far off our proposed course. Despite this I felt we could make the coast of Ireland but might have to be flexible in our destination. At 0900 I wrote in the log 'departed Holyhead towards Ardglass.' This was a distance of 65 nautical miles on a straight course, which would give us an estimated arrival time of 2130. I didn't mind that we would be approaching the coast at dusk because it would be easier to pick out the navigation lights.

After all the weather-borne frustrations of the last few days, it felt good to be under way again. The sea had calmed down and *Shearwater* bowled along nicely. We cleared the Skerries, a group of rocks sharing a name which crops up all around our shores, simply because no one can be bothered to think of anything more original. It means 'group of rocks,' which is true of course. After a couple of hours we approached the separation lanes. These are designated areas established to marshal shipping around constricted coastlines, in this case, as they close the coast heading towards Liverpool docks. Ships heading up the coast must maintain a course of 040° and vessels heading south west a course of 220°. There is a 'central barrier' two miles wide to stop them fighting. Our course took us across the shipping lanes, and so as to dwell for the shortest time in them, we were obliged to cross at 90°. Altering course brought to mind the plight of hedgehogs crossing a motorway, although I suspect the ninety-degree rule doesn't help them much.

I soon had my first chance to try out the AIS. On the screen I saw the image of a large cargo ship approaching us at speed. I could read her name and radio call sign so I thumbed the radio microphone.

'*European Conveyor*, this is yacht *Shearwater*. We are a small sailing vessel two miles ahead of you. Do you have us visible on your radar? Over.'

Back came the reply. '*Shearwater*, this is *European Conveyor*. Yes, I can see you and am altering course ten degrees to starboard. Have a good watch.'

'Many thanks, a good watch to you. *Shearwater* out.'

Before AIS the chances of a small yacht getting a response over the radio from the bridge of a large ship was zilch, but the ability to identify the ship's name and radio call sign has clearly made a difference. I hopped up on deck and waxed lyrical about the wonders of modern technology.

Once clear of the shipping channels I was able to set a final course for Ardglass. The wind was on our port side, but it soon became clear that the tide was pushing us off course to the north. Having abandoned visiting the Isle of Man the last thing I wanted was to get washed up there by accident. Just to be helpful, at this point the wind dropped so we started the engine. Motoring combined with a mid-channel slop induced a lazy roll in *Shearwater*'s motion. Joy held out for about four hours before a ghostly white complexion presaged her succumbing to sea sickness. She looked pretty cold and I persuaded her to go below, armed with a bucket. We tucked her up with a sleeping bag and in between regular bouts of heave-ho she dozed fitfully.

Simon and I yarned away the miles, scoffed food regularly and lamented the fate of our third crew member. The Isle of Man remained in view all afternoon. I hadn't realised until then how visible the island must be from the Irish coast; I had assumed it would be hidden in the middle of the Irish Sea. By the time I'd cooked an evening meal and cleared away the pots, the Mourne Mountains of County Down had framed a deep red setting sun which lit up the Manx hills, now dropping away behind us. Simon took pictures of the dark clouds forming finger silhouettes against the flaming sky. One of them looked for all the world like the outline of Old Father Time on the weather vane at Lord's cricket ground.

When closing the coast on an offshore passage everyone is keen to identify the relevant navigation lights. Lighthouses and navigation buoys each display distinctive light characteristics that a navigator can use to identify them on the charts. We were anxious to make out St John's Lighthouse which guards the headland a few miles south of the entrance to Ardglass harbour. Important lighthouses, such as St John's, display more than one light, each visible at a different distance, so you can determine not only your bearing but your distance off the coast. Or, nowadays, you can just look at the little boat shape on the chart plotter screen. I like to keep my hand in with the old methods so I jotted down the light sequences and, using binoculars, peered over the sprayhood into the darkness.

The lights of St. John's Point eventually obliged and I made an entry in the deck log. Despite all the technology, nothing is as reassuring at night as spotting the sweeping beam of a sought-after lighthouse. As we closed the coast the waves flattened off and *Shearwater* purred along under sails and engine. We enticed Joy to join us in the cockpit for the final approach, the calm sea prompting her recovery. The light winds and punching the tide had slowed our progress and it was pitch black when we crept into the harbour entrance at Ardglass. I had to trust the pilot book that we could access the tiny harbour at low water. This sort of pilotage is both challenging and exciting. It's a bit like solving a mystery, unlocking the clues to gain entrance to a hidden haven, except you can't always have another go if you get it wrong.

As we approached the harbour red, green and white lights flashed their beckoning signals, sometimes disappearing in the orange haze of street lights. When we were close to where the pontoons should have been Simon took up position in the bows, sweeping a spot light across the rocks lying well exposed on one side of the channel. Just when it seemed as though we were running out of water the torch beam settled on the hull of a moored yacht. We stowed the sails and fixed our fenders before rounding up behind a French cruiser. I aimed for a vacant space and throttled back the engine, allowing *Shearwater* to glide alongside. Simon jumped onto the pontoon with our bow line, which action was followed by a strange noise. He later confessed this arose from desperate efforts to avoid falling into the water. There was no need to show off, I thought. It had been a successful passage. We had arrived in another country. We celebrated with a coffee and a drop of the hard stuff, before surrendering to a deep, contented sleep.

When we woke, all was quiet in the harbour. The marina was pretty run down. In the office a wizened old man who I thought was the cleaner turned out to be the manager. He fumbled amongst scraps of paper to find the rate to charge us for the night. Clearly there was to be no discount for arriving in the small hours and leaving at daybreak. I inspected the showers, with taps hanging off the walls and decided I could manage with a quick wash on board. With a bit of luck the full ablutionary facilities of Bangor Marina would avail themselves in the evening.

Joy went to explore the little town and buy some provisions while Simon cooked breakfast and I planned the passage up the coast. We waited a few minutes for Joy to return before concluding either she'd jumped ship or had been abducted, so we ate our eggs and bacon and were about to woof hers when she appeared, perhaps reluctant to give up the security of solid ground. She said there wasn't much to see so we ventured no further ashore and cast off towards Bangor.

Our landfall in Northern Ireland had been a bit of an anticlimax but the bright lights of Belfast beckoned. The sky was very grey and as we set sail we eyed each black cloud rolling off the hills and wondered which would give us a soaking. Much to Joy's relief, the sea was calm and there was enough breeze over the stern quarter to push us along nicely. We were in good spirits.

One of the most useful instruments housed over the companionway is the wind gauge. This displays the direction and speed of the wind over the boat. Only it was under-reading. The wind was gusting over the land, at times pushing our lee gunwale under water but the dial was unmoved. There are other ways to gauge the wind strength. You can note the appearance of the waves; if they resemble white horses you can assume wind strength Force 5, but the instruments are useful to spot a gradual increase in the wind. At the top of the mast three little cups whiz round and send a signal to the read-out. It was all fitted new with the replacement mast and I'd already paid a rigger to go up the mast in Bristol because I was suspicious of the reading. It looked as though it was playing up again, which was tiresome.

The sailing was good and, despite unwelcome attention from squally rain showers, we enjoyed the passage up the coast, passing the entrance to Strangford Lough carving its way inland. The pilot described it as worth a visit. Another time, I thought. Off the north-eastern corner of the coast, barring our course to Belfast Lough, lay the Copeland Islands, complete with numerous boat-wrecking rocks in attendance on all sides. You can give them a broad berth to seaward, which adds several miles to the journey, or sail between the islands and the coast through the Donaghadee Sound. The channel is well-buoyed, and safe, provided you keep a careful eye on the boat's course and allow for any tide which might be sweeping you sideways.

Simon was on the helm and revelled in the responsibility of holding *Shearwater* on a true course. As we cleared the last of the buoys a heavy squall hit us, with driving rain obliterating any view of the coast. It blew through pretty quickly and we had a fast, exhilarating reach into Bangor and the Quays Marina. I was expecting this to be a smart place and we weren't disappointed. The standards in these marinas are a cut above the norm with the bonus that, being owned by the same group as our home port, I was entitled to free berthing. Over the radio we were directed to a place in the harbour lined by imposing tall, bay windowed houses with pastel-washed walls. No doubt they dated back to when Bangor was an important seafaring port. Not that we weren't important. It was Saturday night and *Shearwater* was back on schedule.

Our fourth crew member for the week, Colin, arrived half an hour later on his pal's boat, having sailed down the coast from Larne. Colin is another old acquaintance from Ogston. He's a charming man, very bright, in a boffiny sort of way, and seen by some as being slightly eccentric. On *Shearwater* we had a little drinks party although we did most of the consuming because Colin and his friend Bill had been catching up all the previous evening and most of the night, and confessed to having seen the sun rise. I expected the crew to get wrecked on the last night but didn't know what to make of them arriving in that state at the beginning of the trip. We changed and ambled up into town and ate dinner in a traditional Irish restaurant with leaded lights and Tiffany glass lanterns. On reflection these may have nothing at all to do with Ireland but it was a cosy spot and the fish was good. We talked boats and plans and

had a few more drinks on Bill's boat before retiring to bed. Colin decided to
sleep there which, in view of events later in the week, might have been an act
of mercy on his part

On Sunday we decided to have a day off. The schedule for the week ahead
wasn't too punishing. We were aiming to arrive at Oban by Friday, a sailing distance of 130 nautical miles. We all fancied a visit to the *Titanic* exhibition in Belfast. This was my first day off not imposed through bad weather. The prognosis
for the week ahead looked good with the promise of light winds and sunshine.
We caught the train and spent a couple of hours immersing ourselves in the
proud ship- building history of Belfast and the story of the *Titanic*. The background to the building of the ship, the construction and the events leading up to
the sinking were all explained wonderfully, but nowhere could I find any information as to why this 'unsinkable' ship foundered.

I cornered one of the curators. 'Excuse me; I'm puzzling why there is nothing
to actually explain why she sank?' I asked.

He shuffled from one foot to the other, then said, 'Ah well, it was nothing to
do with the construction or the ship's architect. He designed sixteen watertight
bulkheads running the full depth of the ship. But the owners wanted to maximise the first class living accommodation on the upper decks and so the bulkheads
weren't built high enough. When she took on water they were useless.'

'You won't have that problem on *Shearwater*, will you Rod?' said Colin. But
just to show confidence in their home for the week the crew treated me to a gift
from the souvenir shop, a *Titanic* tea towel.

We took a taxi into the city centre, clocking the powerful sectarian images that
still adorn the gable ends of many buildings. Simon was yearning for a traditional
Sunday lunch so we found a pub serving just that. After lunch we strolled back
through the old docks, where famous old ships and dockyard curios lie amongst
the yuppie apartments and trendy restaurants.

Back on *Shearwater* Colin stowed his gear. I gave Joy the forecabin, to spare
her the nocturnal habits of three blokes and moved to the quarterberth which
lies behind the navigation table in the main cabin. It's comfortable enough once
you've wriggled into place and squeezed your feet alongside the life raft. I was to
regret my chivalry more than once during the week ahead.

That night we were too full to eat anything more but decided to promenade and find a pint of the 'black stuff.' The day before, sailing across Belfast Lough, we'd spotted the clubhouse of the Royal Ulster Yacht Club, looking every bit as imposing as its counterpart in Cowes. What better way to spend the evening, we thought. Alas, we were met at the door by the steward who announced they were just closing. This was at eight o'clock. They must go to bed early, I thought. Next door we found the *Jamaica Inn* overlooking the Lough, with great Guinness, live music and two characters who provided a riot of entertainment. Tony, a retired RUC officer (who at first said he'd have to kill us if he told us what he did) and his pal, John, an estate agent, had been there since lunch-time. The rounds flowed along with the stories, and ribaldry. When we could get a word in we told them our sailing plans and they urged us to visit a beautiful anchorage just down the coast from Oban. We resolved to go there but the next day the closest we could get to remembering the name was 'Pull your brains out', the title we used all week until I found a small anchorage on the chart called Puilladobhrain. Tony and John took a shine to Joy and kept us laughing all evening with their banter. When it was clearly time to go we waved off John, and Tony accompanied us to the marina. We paused alongside his yacht.

'Will you be joining me on board for a nightcap?' he slurred. It had all the makings of a heavy session so we made our excuses and shook hands.

I settled down in my sleeping bag. Colin bustled about getting his bunk ready, dropping the lee board on his toe with a resultant commotion and hopping around the cabin. I drifted off to sleep for only a short time before I became conscious of a deep growling noise. The boat was not moving, so clearly it wasn't the sound from a powerful motor launch arriving late. We had nothing on the boat to make that noise, except it seemed the occupant of the starboard bunk. The sound developed steadily to resemble the growl of an old steam engine labouring to haul a long train of goods carriages up a steep incline. It culminated with a guttural gurgle, a cough and then silence reigned for a few seconds before the cycle began again. I put the pillow over my head, but it was coming light when I finally overcame the snoring.

That was just about the same time as Colin decided to rise. With all the appropriate banging he crashed out of the cabin and headed off for a shower. Simon's phone chose that moment to disgorge a torrent of emails, each accompanied by the appropriate bell or whistle. God, I've got another week of this, I thought.

I struggled out of bed and filled the kettle. On the way to the shower I paused to admire the black guillemots nesting in the harbour walls. Colin strolled up.

'Morning, Rod,' he chirped. 'Sleep well?' I shrugged and managed a half-nod. Bite your tongue, Rod, I thought.

We re-fuelled and departed towards Glenarm, a small harbour mid way along a stretch of sea known as the North Channel. This narrow neck of water separates Ireland from Scotland and through it funnels the mass of tide flowing into the Irish Sea from the Atlantic. The tidal range (the difference in height between high and low water) is up to ten metres and inevitably this produces very strong currents. Get the tide wrong and you could find yourself going backwards or being carried onto the rocks on either shoreline. As the pilot books caution, 'careful planning is required.' I figured that Glenarm would place us far enough up one side of the channel to make sure of carrying the full tide in our favour for the crossing to Scotland.

The sea was flat calm when we motored across Belfast Lough, in company with several other yachts who had the same plan. The sun got the better of the mist as we edged along the steep cliffs of Carrickfergus. Colin offered to make a coffee. After a few minutes he called up from the cabin, 'Rod, the electric kettle seems to be on the blink.'

In the cockpit we stared at each. Simon rolled his eyes. 'It's my fault, Colin,' he said. 'I didn't think the shore power cable would stretch more than a couple of miles and unplugged it before we left.'

Colin didn't reply but we heard the clatter of the hob kettle coming out of the locker and the gas being turned on.

There was no wind but the ebb tide and *Shearwater*'s engine combined to push us speedily over the ground and we covered the twenty miles in time to moor at Glenarm in late morning. We tied up on a pontoon in a tiny harbour created from huge stone boulders. The harbourmaster walked down and introduced himself. He was a very friendly chap. He said there were no restaurants in the town but we could get a breakfast in the high street café. An hour later we staggered out of the said establishment, having sampled the 'Full Ulster Fry.' It seemed to comprise every kind of soda bread soaked in fat with bacon and egg perched on top.

Simon volunteered to go up the mast to investigate the cause of our under-reading wind gauge. I'm getting a little long in the tooth to relish scaling masts and gratefully accepted. We rigged up the bosun's chair. This is a canvas seat, a bit like a heavy duty nappy with a stainless steel loop to which you attach the mainsail halyard, and then clip on the spinnaker hoist as a backup. He climbed in and, armed with some tools and a camera to record the view from the top, beckoned for us to begin winching. After a lot of puffing we hauled an enthusiastic but Ulster Fry laden lump to the masthead. He prodded and poked the cup swivel and shouted down, 'Can't see anything wrong, just seems a bit stiff.' We sent up a bucket with some synthetic lubricant and he squirted the key components. Joy thought it might be fun to tie off the halyards and leave him there for a bit but I was a spoilsport, remembering only too well the circulation strangling, dead leg inducing pressure of the harness, and supervised the careful easing of the ropes to bring our hero back to deck level.

The harbourmaster had come to observe, if only to personally witness any disaster on his watch, while Joy took lots of photographs. They chatted for a bit and she then announced the harbourmaster had said she might like to see the famous Spanish chestnut tree in the cemetery at nearby Cairncastle. He'd drive her to see it. The rest of us wondered if this was the Northern Irish equivalent of 'would you like to see my etchings?' She went off anyway and a bit later returned safely with pictures to prove such a tree existed. Its provenance was even more fanciful, reputedly having grown from a chestnut left in the pocket of a sailor drowned at the time of the Spanish Armada. The harbourmaster told us that samples of the wood from the tree dated back to the 16th century. Who were we to argue?

After all the exertions up the mast Simon decided he needed a nap and the rest of us went off for a walk in Glenarm Forest, once part of the castle grounds, and now a nature park. It was alive with the sounds and smells of spring. A pervading aroma of garlic welled up from the wild plants that stretched away under tall trees that lined the fast flowing river. We trekked along the woodland paths, stopping to listen to birds courting, warning or just revelling in the excitement of the season. At odd places along the route exotic statues had been carved out of the stumps of fallen trees: hobgoblins, dragons and woodland creatures. The river was clear and bright and looked ideal for sport as confirmed when we passed a sign for a salmon fishery. The countryside was delightful and was the first of many places on the trip that I resolved to re-visit in the future, perhaps without the impediment of a boat.

Walking back through the village we wandered along cobbled pavements amongst pretty cottages with a ringside view of the North Channel and in the distance the mountains of the Kintyre Peninsular. In the Main Street we called at the tiny grocers shop to rifle their stock of fresh meat with a view to dining on board, but not before we'd sampled some more Guinness. We phoned Simon to suggest he joined us in one of the pubs, The Coast Road Inn. The decor was old, wooden and cosy, the landlady friendly and the Guinness smooth and tasty. There was only one other person in the bar. She was behaving as though she'd arrived about a week before us. To avoid her attention we took our glasses to a quiet corner and watched as someone arrived to take her home. We rigged up the camera for a pint-bearing portrait and absorbed the atmosphere of the place. It didn't take much imagination to picture the scene when the place was hopping.

The meal on board was very convivial. We chatted about the passage ahead, planning to make Port Ellen, on Islay, our Scottish landfall. The harbourmaster had given us tips about the crossing, advising that, provided we kept a good lookout, we could transit the separation channels off Rathlin Island without performing the ninety degrees dog-leg. It was 36 miles to Scotland.

Seven

cͻ

Shipping Forecast for 24 hours from 06.00 Tuesday 4th June
Irish Sea
Wind east or southeast Force 3 or 4 turning variable later.

I HAD TURNED IN THE NIGHT BEFORE with trepidation, but Simon and I were spared the worst of the 'Darth Vader' sound effects from the starboard bunk. Colin was still up ridiculously early, striding up to the washrooms. We untied at 0745 and motored out in the North Channel. Again there was thick mist which took longer to clear than the day before. I was quietly praying that it would lift before we skedaddled across the shipping lanes, and I must have got through straight away because soon enough the sun appeared in a cloudless sky. Before long we could see the Mull of Kintyre away to starboard, and ahead, on the horizon, the jagged line of Islay and the mountains of Jura.

It was a beautiful day with some real warmth in the sun. At last it felt as though we were heading into better weather. The wind was lighter than forecast. We set the spinnaker and played it for a bit before conceding the need to motor. The islands grew steadily larger, and we snacked and drank rounds of coffee and tea. In this respect Colin and I were as one, content to drink anything that was warm and wet. Joy and Simon had arrived on board nursing bags of mint tea, decaffeinated tea, you name it tea. Making a drink became an art form worthy of a barista in a big city.

From a long way off we could make out the huge grain silo which dominates the sky line of Islay. Port Ellen is at the centre of the Highland whisky distilling industry. Nearly all the malted barley used in its production is grown on the Scottish mainland, unloaded in the harbour and stored in the grain silo. From there it is drawn off to the adjoining plant where it is malted to the recipe directed by the particular distiller before being transported by road and ferries to the island distilleries. A few miles off I hoisted the Scottish courtesy flag which would fly from the starboard cross tree until we re-entered England. Inside the harbour bay we threaded a course around the many rocks littering the approach, tucked in behind the ferry quay and found a berth alongside the community-owned visitors' pontoon.

After clearing away the boat it was time to stroll up into the village. I surveyed the possible eating haunts, Simon and Joy the showers and Colin the loos. Each to their own, I thought. There was only one pub, in the doorway of which two locals lounged, eyeing us suspiciously. It was only five o'clock so we walked past and wandered around the bay. Colin had brought his swimming gear and headed down to the sandy beach, but caught us up pretty quickly having felt the temperature of the sea. A low-pitched drone fanned out from the silo tower and lorries were constantly arriving to load up. As the building was only yards from the mooring pontoon I hoped they turned it off or at least down during darkness—that was if darkness ever fell. The sun was still high in the sky and we sprawled on a patch of fine lush grass, drinking in the charm of it all, until the lure of a beer proved irresistible.

The clientele and staff of the *Islay Hotel* were pleasant and welcoming. We had a splendid dinner and retired to the bar to marvel at the vast array of malts lining the shelves. There must have been over a hundred bottles on display. The barman placed one on the counter.

'How much is that worth?' asked Joy.

'This little beauty will set you back two thousand pounds,' said the barman.

I coughed and ordered a Bell's. Simon put his head round the door and called us back to the pontoon where an enormous grey seal was alongside, begging from a woman as she washed down her fishing craft. We could have leant over and tickled his bristly chin, but it seemed a bit forward on our first meeting. Eventually he grew bored of waiting for a snack and rolled away into the depths.

It was approaching midnight but still only dusk when we settled into our bunks. The grain silo hummed quietly, and Colin returned from his last visit to the amenities and began his complex night concert. Simon's multimedia messaging service maintained a steady flow of communications from Timbuktu, or rather somewhere in a completely different time zone. The next morning when

I was mercifully released from a thoroughly lousy night, I was not in the best of moods. I was starting to feel seriously deprived of sleep. A vague plan had been to investigate an anchorage around the corner just off the Lagavulin distillery and sample our first tour. However, through my red, bleary, sleep-starved eyes the prospect of piloting the boat along a series of complicated compass bearings and rock transits looked daunting. I feigned a weak, nautical reason why we needed another scheme and we motored off up the Sound of Jura towards Craighouse.

The sails were set, but there was no wind and *Shearwater* drifted on the tide flowing up the straits which separate Islay and Jura from the Knapdale Peninsula on the mainland. It was a shame to shatter the silence, but eventually we had to put the motor to work. I sat on the foredeck practising my concertina. I'd brought this along to learn in my spare moments, but it also doubled to serve out retribution on erring crew members, of which Colin featured high on the list at this time. Simon broke the silence by announcing it would be a good place to fish. He unpacked his fishing rod and put on a competent display of sea angling. Despite his casting well ahead of us, our boat speed meant that only the fittest of fish could apply to jump on his hooks. None obliged.

We motored between the rocks loitering at the entrance to the bay and entered Craighouse, the main settlement on Jura, picking up a visitors' buoy. It was warm enough to set up the cockpit table and we lingered over a late lunch, watching the antics of a sailing school boat. The skipper was instructing the crew on picking up a buoy under sail. Despite a few overshoots we were spared their attentions. As Simon cleared away the plates I announced I was planning to get my head down for a snooze.

Colin looked at me. 'I can see you're really embracing this retirement lark, Rod. An afternoon nap now is it?'

I stared at him, sensing my blood boil. 'I'm not sure I would need one every day, were it not for your five hour nocturnal impersonation of Thomas the tank engine.'

He looked taken aback. 'Really? I didn't know I snored. Mind you, my wife has been spending more time in the spare bedroom these days,' he replied. I said nothing and went below, falling into a deep sleep the moment my head touched the pillow. The sound of the dinghy being inflated brought me to.

'Cup of tea, skipper,' said Joy. 'Then we thought we'd go ashore.'

I scrambled out of my bunk, feeling a bit like a child who's missed some of the party. 'Feeling better now?' she winked.

We tied up the dinghy on the pier and walked slowly along the lane around the edge of the bay. For the main settlement on the island it was surprisingly small. The car ferry ceased to run some years ago, now obliging the residents to make their way eight miles along a single track road to catch the small vehicle ferry that runs from Feolin on the south west coast to Islay. In the summer a passenger-only inflatable crosses the straights, but otherwise forget it.

My outburst had created an uneasy silence between us, but walking along the shoreline the beauty of the village thawed relations. We pottered amongst the seaweed-strewn rock pools, like kids on their first seaside holiday. A simple stone cairn commemorated the inhabitants of Jura who had given their lives during the Second World War. A row of low cottages, more like crofts, with corrugated roofs, enjoyed a commanding view over the harbour. A faded interpretation board suggested at one time they were all occupied by retired sea captains, including one of the former captains of the Cutty Sark. I suspected more than one salty hamlet proclaims this history.

'What are your plans for the rest of the week, Skipper?' asked Joy. I reeled off the nights and possible destinations before arriving in Oban on the Friday. She looked at me quizzically. 'What day of the week do you think it is?'

'Tuesday?' I replied.

She shook her head, pitifully. 'Wednesday, I'm afraid.'

We sat in the garden of the village hotel sipping beer, and through the branches of a palm tree observing *Shearwater* bobbing at her mooring. It all seemed a bit surreal. I hurriedly re-jigged the sailing plans. It wasn't a big problem since the overall mileage to Oban wasn't great, but we needed to skip one of my planned overnight stops.

The licensee, a yachtsman himself, was keen to hear about our adventure and added his recommendations to the growing list of must-visit bays and anchorages. In a mellow mood we re-boarded the boat and ate dinner in the cockpit. When we'd finished the sun was still teasing the mountain tops of Jura, putting off bedtime, like childhood memories of a long summer's evening. The sun never did set properly, skimming the horizon in the far northwest only to re-appear again a few hours later in the far northeast.

Early the next morning we took the dinghy back across to the village hoping to experience our first distillery trip, only to find it didn't open until mid morning, by which time we needed to be riding the tide up the Sound of Jura. We grabbed some provisions in the shop, including a bottle of Jura single malt, which later proved most palatable. The dinghy and outboard were stowed and we set off, aiming for Croabh Haven, a yacht harbour boasting all the facilities. With such little wind we had been motoring nearly all the time and I was conscious of the warnings in the pilot books that diesel pumps on the harbour front would become increasingly sparse as we headed north. I had no wish to spend the day lugging fuel cans along the road.

The sea was glassy calm. The only draught was what I squeezed out of the concertina. Amongst the Hebridean Islands the tides run hard, in places fast enough to overcome the power of our little engine, so there was a risk that at times we could be motoring flat out and drifting backwards. Near lunch-time I checked our position and realised that we would not make the southern point of Luing before the tide turned against us. This headland stares across to the Gulf of Corryreckan, a name to strike terror into the heart of any yachtsman, even while snug in his bunk reading a pilot. 'Enough for one day,' I said, and shortened our passage plan by shaping a new course for Crinan.

This proved to be an inspired choice. We reached up into the natural harbour and moored alongside a small floating pontoon below the Crinan boatyard. From there a long fuel line stretched up to a pump. We re-fuelled, then picked up a visitors' mooring buoy. The sun was warm enough to tempt Colin and Joy into a swim. Simon and I wagered at how long they'd brave the chill waters. It was more like watching penguins hop in and out of the sea. I pondered its benefits as a shock treatment for snoring.

We pumped up the dinghy and pottered round to Crinan Harbour. This is a delightful spot created from the lock gates and holding pool at one end of the Crinan canal. Built in 1794 the canal provides a nine mile short cut across the neck of the Kintyre Peninsular. For any yachts heading out of the Clyde transiting the canal avoids a long sail around the Mull of Kintyre. Nowadays it's mostly used by pleasure craft and I felt some regret that our chosen course hadn't brought us that way. I'd have to return another time.

The *Crinan Hotel* is beautifully situated on a raised headland overlooking the bay. Nick, the owner, looking slightly eccentric in bright mustard slacks, was behind the bar whispering to someone we took to be his wife. She turned out to be a distinguished painter. We enjoyed some excellent local seafood. Nestling on her mooring in front of the hotel was a classic varnished two-masted fishing boat. She was built for Nick's family during the war and like all similar craft was obliged to put to sea with the fishing fleet, but never got used for fishing as such. The hotel was the sort of place you'd like to think would provide idyllic comfort, albeit amongst a pervading whiff of faded splendour. We retired to our own faded splendour to watch a fiery sunset and slept like tots. Even me.

It was an early start on Friday. The pilot suggested we needed to be rounding Ard Luing at slack water to avoid the overfalls. As soon as we rubbed the sleep from our eyes we cast off, the kettle went on the hob, and under way we breakfasted on porridge and toast. At Ard Luing, even at slack water, the currents swirled menacingly around the foot of the cliffs. A glance at the instruments confirmed my suspicion. The log was showing *Shearwater*'s speed through the water at five knots, but the read-out from the chart plotter showed us to be making only three knots across the ground. In other words we had a two knots current against us. So much for the predicted time of slack water.

We steered inshore as close as seemed safe, and found some calmer sea. Our speed picked up and we cleared the headland. Originally, I'd planned a course outside Reisa Mahic Phaiden, a small island, to take us out into the centre of the straits where I expected to pick up the benefit of the flood surging up the Sound of Luing. However, a scan of the instruments revealed we were still being headed. On the other side of the straits, only a couple of miles away, the jaws of Corryvrekan, the Great Race, were poised to swallow us up. Its name is derived from the Gaelic meaning cauldron of sparkling seas, which seemed about right. The tidal flow attains ten knots as the sea thunders between Jura and Scarba. To make matters worse the sea bed plunges from thirty to two hundred metres deep along its short length. No wonder the resulting whirlpools and eddies have made this one of the most dangerous sea passages in the world and officially classed by the Royal Navy as un-navigable. And here we were making little progress across its entrance.

I shaped a course inside the main channel, hugging the eastern shore, but avoiding the numerous isolated rocks that threatened to spoil our day. After a tense hour the foul tide relented and our speed over the ground increased to match and then exceed our boat speed. At last we had the tide on our side. In the distance Simon said he could make out a large ferry but after it remained motionless for some time he took up the binoculars and confessed it was actually the island of Fladda presided over by its tall white lighthouse.

'No worries, Simon,' I chortled. 'Anyone could make that mistake.'

After we motored past the island-cum-ferry the seas calmed down and we enjoyed a gentle beat up past Easdale. It was the first sailable wind we'd had all week and it felt great to be able to silence the iron topsail. The coastline fell away to the east and we could free off, bringing the wind more over our stern quarter. *Shearwater* responded to the more favourable wind angle by picking up speed. I made a mess of the chart plotting at first but eventually identified the entrance to the narrow anchorage of Puilladobhrain. This was the anchorage recommended by Tony and John in Bangor as a delightful overnight stop. We could only afford to drop the hook for lunch. Patrolled by several herons we crept up into the shallows at the head of the bay, and anchored between two other yachts. It was hard to imagine how crowded the place could be in the height of summer when, according to the pilot as many as twenty boats settled down for the night.

For lunch Joy treated us to her Welsh rarebit special, with a hint of apple. We necked a can of beer to celebrate finding the bay, and reluctantly weighed anchor to run with the afternoon breeze up Kerrera Sound to the bay of Oban, our final destination for the week. On either bank of the narrow channel a number of magnificent stone houses proudly stood, some fortified and all looking pretty impregnable. Small ferries ploughed back and forth to Kerrera Island. As we approached the head of the Sound and entered the bay of Oban, the breeze picked up and was blowing hard when we rounded up into the marina which lies on the island of Kerrera, within sight of the town on the nearby mainland.

I called up the marina on the radio but got no response. It looked crowded and there was no obvious place for visitors to moor. I began to feel slightly uneasy that there might be no berth. The crew had planned in detail for their journey home, starting with the train from Oban leaving at eight o'clock the next morning. The pilot made clear that there were no alongside harbour berths in the town. I tied up to the marina fuel berth and made my way to the reception to join a queue of yachtsmen at a desk manned by a harassed looking receptionist. Behind her the VHF radio bleated enquiries from further yachts, all ignored. I stepped up to the counter. 'Hi, I was hoping for a berth for the weekend. We're nine point four metres.'

'Well if you go round to 'A' pontoon there might be a vacant berth but I can't promise.'

I ran back down to the boat shouting to the crew to release the mooring lines.

'We need to be quick if we're going to get a berth,' I said, shoving *Shearwater* into gear. The only spare places on A pontoon seemed to those with signs marked 'private berth holder.' I decided to ignore them and fetched up in the most likely looking gap. As we were making good our mooring lines, she of the office was striding down the pontoon.

I smiled at her. 'Are we ok here?' I enquired tentatively.

'Aye, no problem,' she retorted hardly pausing in her step.

We had arrived. Another week, another country and *Shearwater* was gliding north towards Cape Wrath.

We showered away the salt veneer of a few days, put on our smartest gear and headed for the town. A water taxi transports crews from the marina across to the mainland, tying up to a granite slipway at the quayside. On the way over I asked about a boat in the morning to take Joy and the lads to begin their journey home.

'First trip is 08.15,' he said. 'You can book an earlier boat, if you give twenty four hours notice.'

'Ah, we only arrived this afternoon,' I said. 'What's best to do?'

He shrugged, 'There're already booked up for the early boat. All you can do is turn up at seven and see if Jim'll do another trip.'

I relayed this to the others who looked perplexed. As we neared the quayside the taxi skipper beckoned me into his wheelhouse.

'See that ladder there.' He pointed out a rusty iron construction clinging to the side of the high quayside wall. 'If you can't get the water taxi, you might be able to get your boat alongside there and drop your crew off tomorrow.' I nodded somewhat reticently. I could foresee the hassle in taking *Shearwater* over to Oban and then having to re-berth her back in the marina single handed assuming no-one would have pinched the berth in my absence.

On shore Simon went off to buy the rail tickets and we trotted along the quay-side to examine our possible landing spot for the morning. Signs everywhere threatened grim retribution for any unauthorised berthing of vessels.

'Don't worry, folks,' I said. 'If all else fails I can bring you across first thing tomorrow morning.'

This seemed to ease their concern; mine was still simmering—it was the last thing I needed on my changeover day. I had to do some washing, clean the boat and get ready for Jan, Chris and Jinks who were to join me for the next week. Still, tonight was a last night celebration at the end of a good week. Oban, facing west, was bathed in glorious evening sun. We strolled through the streets and booked at a restaurant recommended by the taxi skipper. We couldn't get a table until nine, so we walked up the steep hill to McCaig's Tower, a magnificent reproduc-tion coliseum, constructed in granite by a wealthy philanthropist banker. At the centre of the circle of arches McCaig had planned a museum, art gallery and a central tower. As well as providing work for the local stone masons the structure was intended to provide a permanent memorial for his family. They can't have been too impressed, because as soon as he died all work stopped, but what was built is pretty impressive. We stood outside the arches surveying the view over the bay and the distant islands, shielding our eyes from the intense sun, which had warmed the stone to an uncomfortable heat. Hang on a minute, is this really Scotland, I thought?

The meal was great. We laughed over the incidents during the past week and spirits were high when we rolled out. There was just time to visit Tesco before we caught the last water taxi back. Joy organised the trolley dash and we trudged back to the boat with bags full of provisions for the next week. I'd developed the practice of stocking up several basic meals to heat up should we find ourselves at anchor or in a remote harbour. I purchased a spray midge repellent and we chuckled over the description on the can which read 'It contains a dastardly yet family-friendly formula... works by throwing annoying little bleeders like midges and mosquitoes off your scent. One sniff and they'll head for the hills.' Nothing like telling it as it is!

As we queued on the slipway Colin panicked. 'I've left my glasses somewhere,' he said. We looked at each other.

'Yeah,' said Simon. 'You left them on top of your head.'

On Saturday morning I was up early to cook breakfast. On the pontoon where the water taxi moored, disembarking crew stood around, keen to take their seat. Those who hadn't booked anxiously awaited the arrival of the helm who agreed to come back for another boat-load. Result. Half an hour later I walked back up with team and after hugs and handshakes all round they climbed aboard the water taxi. Joy was a bit emotional, her relief at having survived the week with the lads and her first offshore sailing adventure spilled over.

Eight

લ્જ

WHEN THEY'D GONE I SKIPPED BACK to the *Shearwater*, spoilt for choice in the ways I could spend my day before it all began again. I resisted the temptation to go back to my bunk, despite still feeling the effects of snore-induced sleep deprivation. The washing machine was the first port of call. I chuckled as I slung everything in one wash, imagining the chiding I'd get if Jan had been standing there. 'You must separate out the whites, the smalls, the nylons, the cottons.' It all went in together. I whacked in the soap, went for medium temperature and pressed the button. Couldn't see what all the fuss was about.

I spent the rest of the morning cleaning the boat and sorting out my clothes. I thought I would use the neat little vacuum bags Joy had left on the boat, ignoring the 'knickers and bras' labels. All too soon it was time to catch the water taxi across to Oban. I took my iPad and found a traditional hotel lounge where I ordered tea and scones, really just a subterfuge to utilize their Wi-Fi. I'd set up a blog before leaving home, using a site designed for cruising yachtsmen. I felt slightly self-conscious at first, sharing my adventures alongside the antics of hardened sailors, battling the elements in the Southern Ocean, but my supporters were probably the only people likely to view the blog anyway. I was just re-filling the teapot when the phone rang. It was Chris's wife, Jinks, announcing that they were on the outskirts of Oban. I drank up and wandered down to the harbour front. The benches were full of holiday makers, soaking up the sunshine and licking ice creams—it could have been a scene from any British seaside. I was looking out for Chris's estate car, but nothing appeared. My phone rang again. It was Jan this time asking me where I was. In the background it sounded as though a navigation inspired domestic was unfolding.

I said, 'I'm standing by the large building at the end of the sweep of the first harbour wall, past where the ferries berth. Where are you?' Three versions of their current position assaulted my ear.

Eventually a familiar looking car swung round the corner and three disgruntled travellers emerged, all seeking to engage my attention with disparaging glances towards their companions.

'Have a good journey, then?' I asked. Jinks rolled her eyes, Jan exaggerated a smile and Chris ignored them both. I helped unload the car and pointed out the slipway for the ferry queue. I'd had a tip about a free parking place at the far end of the promenade and Chris and I went off in the car, exchanging consolatory observations about map reading, partners and the world at large. As we parked, in the distance I saw the water taxi setting out across the bay and we had to race it back to the slipway, arriving hot and panting. The cool breeze fanned tempers and sweaty brows and the talk had turned to more cheerful matters by the time we loaded the bags onto *Shearwater*.

Before dinner we strolled up the hill overlooking the marina. Standing on the rocky plateau amongst delicate wild flowers and lush grass we were charmed by the beauty of the place. Below us a classic old wooden yacht was motoring through the glassy sea, heading out towards Mull. In the misty sunset the Highland Isles lay in wait. When the midges had eaten their fill we returned to the boat and I cooked supper. We discussed our plans for the week ahead. In the original schedule I had indicated the Isle of Skye as our destination, but hadn't specified where. Chris and Jinks had assumed it would be Portree, the main harbour on the eastern side. Jinks had made careful enquiries as to the times of buses from there to Fort William and then back to Oban. It all went very quiet when I announced that I preferred Loch Harport on the southwest coast.

'Sailing to Portree means a long flog up the Sound of Sleat,' I said, 'And then I'll be on the wrong side of the island to get out to the Outer Hebrides.'

'But there's nothing at Loch Harport is there?' asked Jinks. 'How do we get back from there?'

I pulled out the map and showed them the road from Portree that ran through Sligachan to meet the road from Loch Harport. I tried to make light of the potential connection issues, which made matters worse. Jinks lost her normally cheerful demeanour and snapped something about a long car journey and now uncertainty about the return. I realised it was foolish to have said anything that night and let it drop. The weather would probably dictate somewhere entirely different anyway. Sleep would provide the necessary balm and we all turned in. Jan and I snuggled up in the forecabin.

Sunday dawned under another cloudless sky. We had a lazy breakfast and sat in the cockpit planning our passage up the Sound of Mull. Everything I had read or heard suggested that a visit to Tobermory, near Mull's northern tip, was an absolute must. The pontoons in the harbour are run by island volunteers and I phoned the harbour office to see if we needed to book a berth.

'It's first come, first served,' said Mary, the duty officer, 'but there should be room for you.'

If it was as popular as everyone suggested, the word 'should' was a little unsettling. Arriving at the end of the day and then having to re-plan the night's anchorage is never ideal but there was no alternative. One pilot book entry for Oban suggested that Tobermory was the last significant settlement between Oban and Stornoway on Lewis. I dipped the diesel tank. There is no fancy fuel gauge on *Shearwater*, just a marked stick you poke down the neck of the tank. It's probably more accurate than a gauge, just not as practical. We had enough fuel for the week ahead, even if we had to motor all the way.

The tide up the Sound of Mull swung in our favour at midday. Jan made some sandwiches while I topped up the fresh water tank, and went to pay at the marina office. The VHF burbled unanswered all the time I was queuing at her desk.

The modest south-westerly breeze filled the sails as we set a course on a close reach across the Firth of Lorne, passing between the tall, proud lighthouses at the entrance to the Sound of Mull. On this heading the boat was almost beating, the sails were sheeted in fairly tight and the *Shearwater* assumed a gentle heel. Small waves disturbed the surface of the sea, but never hindered our progress. It was a perfect sailing day, the sort of day when everyone is itching to take a turn at the tiller.

At this point many yachts turn to starboard to head for Fort William and the Caledonian Canal which stretches north-eastwards across Scotland to emerge on the east coast at Inverness. But there were to be no short cuts for us. Cape Wrath and Orkney held our destiny. The Sound of Mull runs for about twenty miles between the island of Mull and Morvern, which looks like an island but is mainland Scotland. Off Duart Point, on the eastern edge of Mull, Duart Castle stands imperiously protecting the coastline. It was our first sighting of a highland castle, exactly the scenery that comes to mind when imagining a voyage in these waters.

The wind eased in strength and backed to the south which could only mean one thing—the spinnaker. These are the highly coloured sails you see billowing out from the bows of yachts as they sail downwind. Usually flying the spinnaker is accompanied by cursing and swearing as numerous extra ropes are deployed to control the baggy monster. Many years ago Jan, intimidated by many panic-strewn dramas associated with this sail, christened it the 'S' word. But today there was no drama. The new spinnaker pole, rigged to project out from the mast and support the shape of the sail, was eased from its mountings on the front of the mast and the sheets took the strain of the sail as it unfurled. I chuckled in delight at the site of the huge orange and yellow sail silently powering us up the Sound. We exchanged greetings with other yachts all enjoying the marvellous sailing conditions. At one point we steered to the edge of the Sound to give clear passage to a Caledonian Macbrayne (CalMac) ferry steaming earnestly towards a Highland harbour. With its black hull, white superstructure and bright red funnel it looked like a grand old Cunard liner of yesteryear. It wasn't hanging about, so a wide berth seemed appropriate.

The wind died away in the late afternoon so reluctantly we dropped the spinnaker and cranked up the engine. From all directions yachts were converging on Tobermory. No one will openly admit as much, but inevitably you find yourself nudging up the engine revs to race other vessels, fearing they might claim that last berth. As we entered the harbour a forest of masts confirmed my concerns. I put the engine into idle and gently coasted *Shearwater* towards the shore where a woman with a hand held radio and a clipboard was patrolling the marina. I called her up and, unlike at Kerrera, she answered promptly. On hearing *Shearwater* was a bilge keeler, with a shallow draft, she directed us to an inside berth. We prepared the fenders and were soon secure.

It was a dreamy, balmy evening. The soft sunlight washed over the multi-coloured walls of the cottages and shops lining the harbour front. We sat in the cockpit sipping gin and tonic, and kept pinching ourselves. Was this really an evening in Scotland? We'd planned to eat ashore but it was too blissful to drag ourselves off the boat, so I lit the oven and rustled up some pizza and salad. At ten o'clock

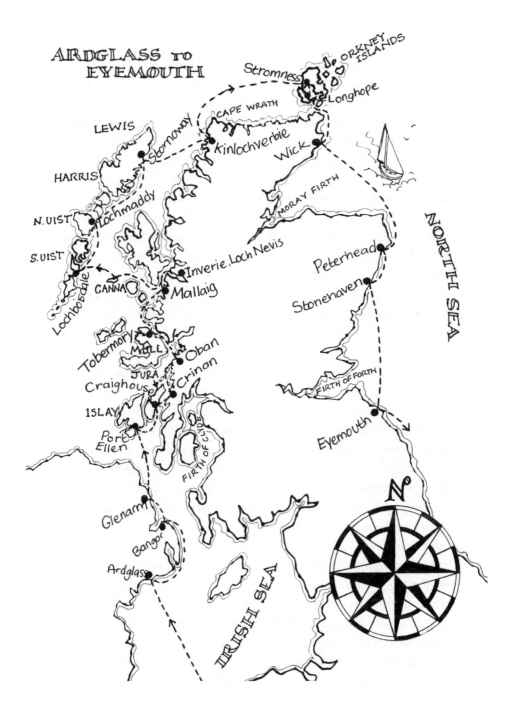

it was still light and warm and it seemed as though it would never get dark. Only tiredness and utter contentment coaxed us into the cabin and to bed.

The next day was for exploring ashore. It was one of those days I would grow to cherish. A day when there was no need to spring out of bed early to scrutinize the shipping forecast, no need to look up the tides and do all the passage planning. Today we could all play at holiday makers. We strolled ashore, admired the posh new visitor centre with its exhibition of life, work and wildlife on Mull. We toured the distillery and were so taken with the images of the beach in the promotional film that we decided to organise our own tour of the island, and I hired a car from the garage on the harbour side. We grabbed a few snacks from the boat and set off to inspect the hinterland of this charming island. Immediately the scenery looked less harsh than the rocky mountains of Jura, the hamlets more complete. It was altogether a busier place. I learned that prior to the Highland Clearances it was home to more than 10,000 people. Nowadays this has shrunk to 2,000, a few more with tourists each summer.

We bounced along the narrow single-track lanes dropping down to the curve of Calgarry Bay, a classic Hebridean beach, where silky-fine sand meets crystal clear blue sea. The dunes were awash with sea grasses, bright wild flowers and nesting sand martins. The tiny tea-room was a shiplap shed with an upturned boat as a roof. The sea looked inviting, but a paddle along the foreshore was bracing to say the least, and we retired to eat lunch sitting on the sun-warmed rocks. The island was much bigger than we first thought, the second largest island in the Hebrides. We completed a circular tour of its northern half, stopping for mugs of tea in a cottage overlooking Loch Tuarth. We thought it must have been their first season, and we their first customers judging by the way they fell over themselves to serve four teas and some biscuits on a plate. In the evening we failed to get into the highly renowned fish restaurant which overlooks the fisherman's pier. They offered to sit us outside but the sultry heat of the previous evening must have been a passing treat, because the sunset invoked a chilly wind and eating dinner in a windproof jacket didn't appeal. We found a meal in a harbour-front pub which was a poor substitute.

The visitor centre had an all-singing and all-dancing computer link to weather forecasts displayed on a large screen. This foretold of a wet and miserable day on the Tuesday and some strong winds during the week ahead. It seemed unfair to have enjoyed such a beautiful couple of days only for it to revert to 'traditional' Scottish weather. Chris and Jinks wouldn't mind, being hardy mountain walking types, but Jan has always resisted sailing in Scotland because of the weather and I was desperate to show her its better side.

On Tuesday the sound of rain drumming on the forehatch woke me. It can be just as irritating when the weather forecast is spot on. I turned over and went back to sleep, hoping when I next stirred it would all be good again. The enforced encampment in South Wales had taught me to be patient with the weather. If I'd been on my own I could have pottered about the boat or skulked in one of the cafes on the waterfront and read the paper. Eventually I could no longer ignore the sound of the kettle and stirring bodies in the main cabin. I knew Chris and Jinks would be keen to sail and, resigned to the fate of a wet weather passage, I reluctantly dragged myself out of bed. A bowl of porridge served only to remind me that summer had been put on hold. I hauled on my waterproof jacket and ventured out into the misty dank morning.

When I studied the screen in the visitor centre the forecast hadn't improved. The wind was no worse, just uninviting, a south-westerly Force 4 or 5 with squally showers. Ahead of us lay Ardnamurchan Point, as chilly and foreboding as its name suggests. A solitary lighthouse on the tip of the peninsula guides vessels past the most westerly point on the British mainland. The pilot book gave all the usual grim details of overfalls, squally winds and rocky graveyards for ships and mariners who get it wrong. It could all have sounded quite romantic were it not for the necessity to sail around it on our passage towards Skye.

I brooded over the charts and pilot book. Loch Harport on Skye looked pretty sheltered, but apart from a distillery there was nothing much there if we became storm bound. So I announced we would abandon it as our weekend destination and head towards Mallaig, on the mainland. This met with the universal approval of the crew, heading off any threat of mutiny. I suggested for our evening target the island of Rhum. The wind was forecast to back round to the south-west, which would make anchoring in the bay on the eastern side a suitable overnight stop. The earliest we could take advantage of the tidal stream was after lunch, so I had the morning to pore over the charts and do the reverse of a rain dance.

My witch-doctoring didn't work but I could see Chris and Jinks were itching to set off, so I clambered into my foul weather gear, which almost matched my mood. Jan was surprisingly upbeat as she pulled tight the hood on her jacket. My sea boots felt strangely uncomfortable. I looked down to observe I was wearing two left feet. Silly me, I thought until I realised that there was no right boot in the wet locker. One of my crew the week before had gone home with it. Having someone else's left was hardly a consolation. A quick text soon elicited the relevant confession. Simon's ears must have been burning. I asked him to contact Alan, one of the crew for the following week, who could bring my other boot with him.

We cast off and motored out of the bay into the wet murk. Outside the calm of the harbour the wind piped up and we set a full main and genoa. The rain wasn't too bad, if you like sailing in that sort of thing, and our spirits were raised by a professional display from two dolphins who escorted us across the delightfully named Bloody Bay towards Ardnamurchan. As we approached the point the waves increased and white horses tumbled off the crests, whipped along by the freshening breeze. It seemed sensible to give the headland a good offing and gradually the lighthouse appeared through the mist on our starboard beam. Mugs of tea arrived in the cockpit at the same time as the decision to reef the mainsail. Most impressively, throughout the process Jinks managed to keep hold of my mug without spilling a drop. It was traditional for vessels rounding the point to display a sprig of heather from their bow to show the natives that they were arriving in peace. It must have been the bad weather or something but there were no gypsies or other pedlars rushing out to sell us a bunch. I said we'd have to rely on gifts from the treat box if things got a bit tense.

Rhum is one of a group of sparsely inhabited islands known as the Small Isles along with Muck and Eigg, both of which lay directly on our intended course. We had to either harden up, or ease away below the islands and then harden up on the other side. These strange sailing terms don't do justice to their importance when a boat is clawing to windward. Ground lost carelessly is hard won back. We opted to harden up and tack along the eastern coasts of Muck and then Eigg. Visibility was very poor and only the odd glimpse of the islands' rocky crags penetrated the drizzle. Sailing on this course we were advancing along a lee shore, in other words the land was downwind of us. This is always potentially dangerous because if anything goes wrong you will get blown ashore rather than safely away from the land. I kept a close eye on the chart plotter, tracking our course northward, and quietly breathed a sigh of relief when the tip of Eigg passed astern.

It was growing dark. The wind had not backed as forecast, and although we were now able to free off and sail speedily downwind to Rhum I suspected when we arrived we would find the anchorage still raked by the northerly wind. The pilot book described the holding ground as poor, and unless the wind changed direction or abated it would not be a safe place to spend the night. We could always take a look but I feared that if we arrived and found the anchorage to be untenable it would be a long slog to windward to the most sheltered harbour at Mallaig. The choice was obvious but it seemed a bit premature on day three of the week to be heading to our final destination. We discussed the options and agreed that Mallaig was the best choice. If the weather turned bad the harbour would offer more distractions ashore, and during the remainder of the week, if the gales failed to materialise, we could always explore the nearby lochs.

We tacked and I set a course north east to raise the lighthouse set on the rocks outside Mallaig harbour entrance. We had about 10 miles to run, which would have us arriving well after dark. I called the harbourmaster who confirmed there were plenty of berths on the visitors' pontoon.

'Just pick a spot and I'll see you in the morning,' he said. He gave me the code to get through the locked access gate. You never know when you might want to go clubbing.

Somewhat bedraggled, we arrived outside the harbour at Mallaig, and tip-toed carefully around the rocks strewn across the entrance. The smell of fish wafted across from the quayside as we motored slowly inside, struggling to pick out the pontoons against the street lighting which glared out from the harbour wall. The pontoons appeared and Chris hopped off at the bow to make us fast. Earlier Jan had lit the oven, and when I turned off the engine she opened the hatch, releasing the delicious aroma of steaming food. The heavens opened as we stowed the sails so we made everything secure in double quick time, anxious to shed our soaking gear and get out of the weather. It's always a temptation to blunder, fully clothed, down into the cabin but that inevitably results in damp cushions. We stuffed the wet gear under the sprayhood and dived below.

It was nice and snug in the cabin, and after hot food and red wine we whiled away the rest of the evening chatting and relishing our landfall. Outside, the sodium lighting refracted through a steady drizzle to turn the quay, crowded with fishing boats, into an impressionist painting. It was like watching an art-house film. Suddenly the deep rumble of powerful engines filled the air and we witnessed the swift departure of the lifeboat, causing me once again to pause and reflect on the sea's begrudging tolerance of all who sail on it. But we were securely moored in a sheltered harbour and enjoyed a carefree night.

The next morning we got up late, and a call of nature directed me to the harbourmaster's kiosk at the head of the pontoon. I asked where the toilet and shower block was located. He pointed to a decrepit building along the quayside.

'Ah, we haven't got any showers yet. There's just the public convenience over there.'

'Oh ok. Any suggestions for getting a shower?' I asked.

'Well the café in the town has some on the first floor. Not sure of the price.'

I returned to the boat and imparted this little snippet, which didn't go down too well. Jan went to investigate and came back, rolling her eyes. She said the toilets were very much in the 1950's style, but lacking the gleaming brass work and pristine varnished wood. I looked again at the 'Welcome Anchorages' booklet I'd picked up in Holyhead, which to date had faithfully advised on harbour and anchorage facilities. The entry for Mallaig owed more than a little to poetic licence, opening with the lines 'Mallaig Harbour's new yachting facilities…' Accompanying the description for Mallaig was a host of little icons boasting all manner of yachting amenities. Never mind, at least they had a pontoon.

I offered to cook a slap-up breakfast. As it was now clear that this would be the final port for the week, Jinks went off to investigate their means of escape. She came back from the tourist information office giggling. Apparently the exchange had gone something like this:

JINKS: Good morning, I was wondering if you've got a timetable for the buses from here to Fort William?

ONE TOURIST OFFICE GUY TO THE OTHER: I keep on telling them we need timetables. We're always being asked for this. I've told them countless times.

JINKS: Could you possibly look them up for me? We're planning to travel on Friday.

TOURIST OFFICE GUY: Well, let me see. I'll just get the details. (He opens a large scrapbook and thumbs the pages). Ah yes, there's just one a day, it leaves at eight in the morning.

We laughed. 'It wouldn't have been a very big timetable would it?' she said.

The forecast for the day was better than predicted; no gales, just fresh winds and squally showers. Typical holiday weather I supposed. Chris fancied visiting Inverie in Loch Nevis and in particular the *Old Forge Inn*, an award-winning gastro-pub which is reputedly the most remote tavern in Britain. According to the 'Welcome Anchorages' booklet free mooring buoys were available to customers. I phoned to check on this and said we'd arrive later in the afternoon. I couldn't reserve a spot but at least the buoys did exist. Before leaving Mallaig I visited the harbourmaster again to book a berth for the weekend, not wishing to repeat the uncertainty of Oban.

We sailed out of the harbour, round the jagged rocks, which in daylight looked no friendlier, and decided to cross the Sound of Sleat to anchor for lunch on the south-west corner of Skye. The sea had calmed and *Shearwater* romped along with all the enthusiasm of an exercising horse. A dark, brooding sky draped its clouds across the Cuillin Ridge, a magnificent range of rocky mountains forming the backbone of the island. Gannets wheeled overhead as we tacked briskly down the coast towards a sandy bay at the very tip of the island, the Point of Sleat. A group of seals were basking on the rocks at one side of the bay and some kayakers had hauled their craft up the beach and stared hard, perhaps aggrieved at us encroaching into their isolation.

We dropped the anchor in crystal clear water, where silver fish darted to and fro under the boat. I had a real sense that we were getting into wilder waters where, untamed by man, nature flaunts its wares. We scanned the cliffs hoping to spot a sea eagle, thought to be extinct thirty years ago, but reintroduced with great success. The wind was bitterly cold, and wearing full sailing gear and woolly hats we huddled in the cockpit in the shelter of the sprayhood; this was a far cry from the balmy heat two days earlier.

Lunch tasted good in the fresh salt air and we warmed our hands clasping coffee mugs. It seemed a shame to leave so quickly but the Old Forge beckoned and we weighed anchor to run before the wind which had finally backed round to the south west. On the way towards Loch Nevis I thought I'd try out my new fishing gear. Dave had been convinced our failure to date was due to not getting the hooks deep enough into the sea. They just flitted across the surface. On my visit home I'd bought some paravanes—delta shapes that drag the line and hooks down to the depths where the fish feed. It had been as cheap to buy four as one, which was just as well, because when I rigged up and launched the first attempt the paravane dived steeply beneath the waves dragging my line off the screaming reel until it reached the end and snapped. Amid giggles of mirth from the crew, I ruefully surveyed the empty reel. Another victory for the fish.

In Loch Nevis we picked up one of the last available moorings in the shallow bay off Inverie. The lights of the *Old Forge Inn* twinkled in the gloomy dusk, and low cloud hung over Loch Nevis. It was tempting to remain on board to eat but we'd come to visit the pub, so we inflated the dinghy and kitted up in wet weather gear, packing our fine dining clothes in rucksacks. The wind was enthusiastically blowing into the anchorage, whipping up the waves, so choosing a sheltered landing spot was important. We opted for a wide slipway in the lee of the fisherman's quay.

We needed to get close enough to step ashore without securing a boot full, but not so close as to mangle the outboard propeller.

The quayside did its job and we hopped out without mishap and carried the dinghy clear of the water's edge. Outside the pub we stripped off our lifejackets and sailing gear, but we needn't have bothered with any fancy clothes. Although billed as a gastro-pub (whatever that means), the *Old Forge* catered for outdoors types, with solid wooden tables and bench seats, the customers resplendent in checked shirts and walking trousers. Numerous musical instruments hung round the bar with a sign inviting guests to take one down and have a go. I've never played a fiddle so thought I'd spare our fellow diners. Interspersed with the instruments, deer antlers protruded from the walls, but they looked completely unplayable. The meal was standard pub fare but it was a jolly night and worth the trip ashore. We negotiated our return without drama and settled down for a lumpy night, *Shearwater* rocking and rolling at her mooring. I wouldn't have liked to have been there in a decent blow.

In daylight, on a brighter day, we could see the extent of the village. It didn't look particularly remote but Chris explained that the road serving the community ran for 10 miles up the side of the Loch and then just petered out. Any access by land necessitated a lengthy trek on foot around the head of the inlet. The only regular communication with the community was by boat, and we saw a steady stream of vessels transporting provisions and passengers who were embarking on a week's walking in the wild. We decided to sail to explore the upper reaches of the loch. The breeze was good, the sea had calmed and *Shearwater* relished the opportunity to show us her performance. We sailed up the loch amongst the sweeping mountain scenery, marvelling at remote farms, and settlements where, for some obscure reason, someone had chosen to live. We saw ruins of abandoned homes, perhaps once owned by victims of the clearances.

At the head of the loch it became shallow so we gybed round to return. The wind began to head us, making for an energetic beat, tacking relentlessly from shore to shore, testing the resolve of the crew. It requires a particular stamina, and upper body strength, to repeatedly wind the winches and tame the genoa sheets. The trick is to watch the sail and, as soon as it flogs across to the new tack, pull like mad on the sheet to get in as much slack as possible before the sail draws. Get it right and there's only a bit of winching. Leave it too late and you've a long grind ahead. It was a fun way to spend the morning, if you like that sort of thing. We ate lunch under way, and in early afternoon moored up in Mallaig, journey's end for this week.

As it was now Thursday, and the forecast didn't look special for the rest of the week, Chris suggested it would help if they began the journey south the next day. After the bus to Fort William, then the train back to Oban, they had to drive with Jan back to Derbyshire, and finally carry on to Devon the next day. It made sailing to the Outer Hebrides look easy. Jan and Jinks went to explore the showers at the café and came back snorting with indignation.

'Four pounds for a shower,' Jan raged. 'And he said we couldn't share one.' I feared one of those embarrassing strip-downs on the foredeck, but fortunately the chilly breeze was deterrent enough.

'And forget the laundry,' said Jinks. 'The guy in the café said it was a myth put about by the marina. He said you could get a shower up the hill at the swimming baths. We walked all the way up there only to find it was closed.'

I was going to say they didn't smell too bad, but thought better of it. I suggested we should walk into town to buy some nice food for a last-night meal on board. Mallaig is renowned for its fish smokery. We followed our noses and were just in time to find still open the fisherman's equivalent of a farm shop. They were emptying the counters but didn't pass up the chance to sell us some fresh scallops and bass. Jinks announced that Chris was a dab hand at preparing these and so he proved to be. *Shearwater* boasts a good sized double-leaf dining table and snuggled down in the cabin it can be made very comfortable. Most of the memorable meals I enjoyed on the trip were those we prepared on board. We spent the evening reflecting on what had been a good week. Even Jan said she'd enjoyed her sailing.

Nine

എ

THE NEXT MORNING I PREPARED KIPPERS and fed up the crew before accompanying them to the bus stop. I hugged Jan goodbye, with the promise to be home in time for her birthday. The bus arrived and I waved them off, and then walked back to the boat. The next crew was not due to arrive until Saturday afternoon. I had a free day. I hadn't updated the blog that week so I called into the harbourmaster's office.

'Morning. I was wondering how I could access the Wi-Fi?'

There was a pause. 'Ah, we don't have any Wi-Fi yet. You could try one of the cafés up in town, or if you walk round to the other side of the bay, when the Calmac ferry comes in you might be able to piggy back their Wi-Fi.' Sitting amongst the seaweed on the rocks didn't sound conducive to considered reporting. I realised it was yet another of the harbour guide icons to be ignored. I collected my iPad, wandered into town to discover a café displaying 'free Wi-Fi here' and ordered a coffee. The free Wi-Fi turned out to be some complicated service requiring me to sign up for goodness knows what and when I had navigated through a lengthy online courtship it spat me out before I could upload the blog entry. By then my coffee was cold.

This frustrating start to the day then took a turn for the better. On the way out of the café, amongst the host of tourist leaflets on a rack by the door, I espied one for the *Jacobean*, the famous steam train service running from Fort William to Mallaig. As luck would have it, I could take the return trip to Fort William that afternoon. I phoned and booked a first class ticket. It was an eye watering fifty five quid, for which I got a cup of tea and a biscuit. The return on the normal service was a mere nine pounds.

If I was playing at being a holiday maker, and travelling first class, I needed a spruce up. I packed my wash kit and, ignoring the temptation to recklessly splash out a further four pounds at the cafe, I trotted up the hill to find the swimming pool. It was open. I paid a pound and got a towel, which was just as well as I'd overlooked that item. I stowed my gear in the locker and armed with a towel and shower gel followed the signs through a door. The full expanse of a delightful community swimming pool hove into view, with the showers at one end in a small shallow alcove. It hadn't occurred to me that I might need swimming trunks. I hesitated but then realised for once my timing was spot on. It was approaching lunch time and the pool was deserted.

I nipped into the shower. This shouldn't take long, I thought. Wrong. There were four showers arraigned along an open wall. When I pressed the button on the first of these it shot out steaming hot water, causing me to jump back in shock, saving my hide from a scalding but exposing my nether regions to view from the pool. I hopped along to the next shower and tried again. It took a few seconds for the spray to attain full heat, and I used this narrow opportunity to wet my skin. I then jumped backwards, into view, and then back again to repeat the procedure at the next shower head. In this fashion, performing a soapy, naked, hokey cokey I completed my ablutions and retreated hastily to the sanctuary of the men's changing room.

'Have a nice shower, Mate?' said the guy at the desk when I returned the towel. I smiled weakly. Back on *Shearwater* I changed into my best tripper gear and wandered up to the station where the *Jacobean* was waiting, contentedly hissing and steaming. Enthusiasts with khaki rucksacks strode up and down the platform, anxious to capture every angle on camera. I found my way to seat number 4 in the first class carriage and sank down into the plush maroon velvet upholstery. Immediately I felt as though I had strayed into a set for an Edwardian adventure film. At the appointed hour there was a shrill toot from the engine and we puffed slowly out of the station, with clouds of sweet-smelling, steamy smoke wafting through the carriage.

My companions eyed me suspiciously. They had all bought a return ticket and were wondering what sort of cheap skate only took the trip back to Fort William. They didn't probe further and I chose not to volunteer my secret. It might have involved a conversation lasting the whole journey. Sat opposite was an elderly American woman, with a thick accent, sporting enough expensive jewellery to explain how she could afford to treat her teenage grandson to a European tour.

She was a gnarled old bird, who knew the tourist angle on everything. When the tea trolley rattled towards her, she turned to her ward and said, 'I couldn't eat another thing Charlie, but make sure you get mine.' They chatted about this place and that, reeling off the names of European top-ten places one must visit.

'How long will it take us to get to Edinburgh from Fort William?' asked Charlie.

'Oh I should think about an hour. It can't be far,' she said. I raised an eyebrow, but got away with it.

I was sat by the window which made taking photographs a bit awkward. Every scene was accompanied by the reflection of a ghostly mug shot of me. The chap in the aisle seat offered to swap. He'd taken all the pictures he needed on the outward journey. I got up and stood in the door lobby, and leaned out of the window, grinning from ear to ear as I snapped the train chugging slowly up the winding incline to the station at Glenfinnan. The train ground to a halt and I think they topped up the water tank or perhaps just mopped the engine's sweaty brow. It was here that Bonnie Prince Charlie summoned a meeting of the clans to enlist their support for the invasion of England. Our arrival passed off without incident and we began our descent, the locomotive fairly rattling along the track like the proverbial runaway train. We steamed across the magnificent arched viaduct made famous in so many films. Through the branches of spring-fresh trees I caught the occasional glimpse of rocky inlets and lochs fringed with golden sand. Another time, I hoped.

The track levelled out and we cruised along the banks of Loch Eil, coasting into Fort William. I just had time to walk to the end of the platform, and buy a bar of chocolate before boarding the standard Scot Rail service back to Mallaig. Although the train lacked the glamour of the *Jacobean*, and the engine hauling it burped along in the manner of heavy diesels, the driver still took the time to halt at special views to enable steerage class to enjoy the scenery. For the first time on my voyage I'd enjoyed being a proper holidaymaker. I cooked a ready meal on board and slept like a toddler after a busy session on the beach.

Saturday was changeover day. Jan and Jinks had already established the absence of a laundry, so my tasks centred on preparation for the next leg. We would be sailing to the Outer Hebrides. The pilot books suggested that food shops might be in short supply and fuel might be problematic. It felt as though we were about to embark on the more adventurous part of the trip. Even the overly optimistic harbour guide didn't claim any alongside re-fuelling facilities so I went off to locate the chandlers, which until recently had only served Mallaig's fishing fleet. In place of shiny stainless and chrome fittings the shelves were lined with heavy galvanised iron blocks, and huge iron shackles. On the floor lay coils of thick polypropylene rope. I bought a large fuel can and paid for twenty litres of diesel before leaving with a chitty and directions to the fuel store.

I turned the corner to see a vast storage tank that wouldn't have been out of place in a refinery. I assumed there hadn't been a misunderstanding and dialled the number on the shabby notice board. Five minutes later a truck roared up disgorging a boiler-suited character who glanced at my receipt, took the can and disappeared through a gate. He re-emerged a few minutes later dumping the container at my feet with a heavy thud.

'You going far?' he enquired, the only words he'd uttered so far.

'Just back to the marina,' I replied, hoping this might elicit the offer of a lift.

'Oh aye, not far then. Have a good trip.'

With a grin and a wave he got back in his truck and roared off. Mental note to self: Need to tone down the subtlety of hints up here.

Twenty paces, pause, transfer can to other hand. Take a deep breath, lug it another twenty paces, pause, switch hands, swear under breath, twenty paces, and pause to mop brow. On the way back I passed and exchanged knowing glances with other yachties carrying empty fuel cans. Back on board I topped up the tank, scrutinising the funnel filter for any signs of sediment. The nightmare of engine failure, in this case from dirty fuel, continued to haunt me. Of course there was no logical reason why diesel from an enormous bunker was any more likely to be contaminated than fuel from a quayside pump, but somehow the recent elevation of Mallaig from hardy fishing port to 'all mod cons' yacht haven seemed only partially complete.

I cleaned the boat, stocked up in the local supermarket and settled down in the cockpit with a sandwich and newspaper. There was a steady buzz of activity around the marina. Motor yachts unloaded holiday makers at the end of their week's isolation in the islands and lochs, and took on provisions before boarding the next customers who stood waiting on the pontoons, sporting huge rucksacks, wet suits, climbing gear and the like. A splash and a glint of sunlight drew my attention to the stern of a fishing boat moored across from *Shearwater*. A sleek shiny otter had hopped onto the stern platform and was munching a newly caught fish. It cautiously peered around the boat before standing on its rear legs to investigate the cockpit, hoping to find left over scraps. Disappointed, it slid back into the sea and dived out of view. What a privilege to have witnessed that, I thought.

My phone rang. It was the new crew; Geoff and Mike from my village and Alan, an old sailing acquaintance from Ogston. They were in Fort William and had booked a taxi in preference to the train. Within the hour my new week would begin. I felt a bit like a hotel proprietor expectantly awaiting the arrival of his new guests. Geoff and I went back a long way. Most of our exploits had been land-based, skiing, golf and the like, although over the years he has joined me for the odd sailing trip. What he calls 'a little jolly.' It was only a chance conversation that had led him to sign up for this trip. I hoped the wilds of Scotland wouldn't prove too 'full on.' I knew Mike had done a bit of sailing, chartered in the Med a few times, but didn't really know the extent of his experience. Alan would be fine.

When they arrived I helped them down the slipway and we loaded their gear. Alan presented me with my right sea boot, but was also holding another one.

'What's that?' I asked.

'It's Simon's other boot. You asked him to give me your boot, so I asked him what size he was and realised I didn't need to buy a pair. He's lent me his for the week.'

'You might struggle there,' I replied.

'Why?'

'Because Jan took his left boot back to Derbyshire.'

Alan looked a bit crestfallen. We fell about at the thought of sea boots criss-crossing the country desperate to be reunited with their owners.

'Never mind,' I said. 'It might not rain much.'

We found a pub and over a pint I recounted my adventures to date and the plans for the week ahead. The final destination was Stornoway, on the northern end of Lewis in the Outer Hebrides. From there the crew would retreat via the ferry to Ullapool and take the coach back to Fort William, where Alan had parked his car. The weather looked fair for a couple of days, with the threat of some rough stuff later in the week. Alan was anxious not to end up in some remote harbour because the following week he was due to take part in a classic car rally in the Isle of Man. I wished him more luck than I'd had getting there.

We cast off the next morning, as the sun begrudgingly began to peer between the clouds. The wind was reticent so, after we set the sails, more for the practice than anything else, the increasingly trusted Bukh chugged away and we headed off towards the Outer Hebrides. I ran through the safety briefing, pointing out the lifebelt, inflatable dan-buoy and the nearest exits. So far on the trip I had made clear the availability of lifejackets and harnesses but only insisted on them being worn at night or when the sea conditions made them obviously necessary. The RNLI runs a constant campaign, pointing out that lifejackets are useless unless worn, which is incontrovertible, but somehow on a flat calm sea it seemed a bit over the top to insist on their use.

We headed towards Canna, the most western of the Small Islands. The pilot book described it as an inviting anchorage where in recent years the local authority has placed a number of visitors' mooring buoys. This is probably my favourite form of overnight mooring. You can enjoy all the privacy and freedom of being at anchor without the hassle of organising the hook to be safely secured in the sea bed. With anchoring you have to worry about getting the right amount of chain down, not swinging too close to other yachts and then hauling it all up again the next morning. A lot of old salts pontificate about not knowing the security of the chain on a strange mooring and the freedom of using your own anchor, but personally, as Jan puts it, 'Rod would rather spend the night on a buoy.'

The wind never showed but the sun made up for it, with clear blue skies treating us to marvellous visibility, revealing the magnificent scale and beauty of the islands. The horizon to the north was dominated by Skye, and on our port side the island of Rhum slid past. Crystal blue sea sparkled in our wake and the salty air smelt deliciously fresh. At the foot of the tall cliffs on the north-western end of Rhum the rusty wreck of a fishing boat lay sprawled on the rocks. It didn't look that old, jarring us into the realisation that we were never far away from a different weather pattern, cruel enough to despatch a sturdy steel hulled vessel to a watery grave.

I peered through the binoculars searching out the entrance to Canna harbour. It's often impossible to see an entrance until close in, the rocks and sand-bars keeping their secrets until the last moment. A gangly beacon on a pole on one side and a light house perched on the clifftop on the other beckoned us onward until the entrance opened up to reveal a few yachts contentedly nuzzling mooring buoys. We dropped the sails, waved to some sunbathing seals at the entrance, and picked our spot.

The pilot book didn't exaggerate the beauty of the place. The harbour nestled in a natural bay surrounded on three sides by gentle rocks coated in lush grass and wild flowers. We relaxed in the cockpit watching each arrival. I spotted a yacht I'd been alongside in Oban, the skipper keen to get out his dinghy and row ashore with his dog, which had all legs crossed. Without the urgency of a canine ship mate we inflated our dinghy and followed. At the head of a long slipway stood a tiny cottage which served as a harbourmaster's office, information point and store. Inside, notices proclaimed the whole place ran on an honesty basis. Mooring fees, books and tourist knick-knacks were all paid for by feeding money into the appropriate box. Mike treated the boat to a book on Scottish birdlife and we picked up leaflets explaining the island's importance as a bird sanctuary.

We wandered to the head of the bay to where a low roofed cottage housed a small café. The original plan was to eat on board but we were all so entranced with the charm of the island that we elected to sit outside, sipping bottled beer and sampling the dish of the day. Our hosts were a young couple from Prague who'd answered an advert for someone to run the café for the season. They'd only been there a couple of weeks and said it was a bit boring. Their apathy seemed to have rubbed off onto the food which had all the appearance of a supermarket ready meal, but it was tasty enough nonetheless. As we sat in the warm evening sunlight, nothing could have detracted from our sheer delight at being there.

On a low hill at the far side of the anchorage there was an isolated chapel, and after we'd eaten and supped enough we took the dinghy over to explore. One of the leaflets suggested we might find puffins nesting on the far headland, but as we wandered across the soft thick grass we only found rabbits in their hundreds. On the foreshore petulant terns wheeled overhead to warn us off their nest sites. A few years ago the island was completely overrun with rats which had threatened the bird population, and were eradicated only after an earnest campaign. I wondered whether the rabbits posed a similar threat, and later discovered they are also to be culled. It goes to show that, unthreatened by natural predators, some species overdo it to the point of signing their own death warrant. It might apply to us before long. With *Shearwater* dreamily resting on her mooring we retired to our bunks, happy bunnies.

On Monday morning the weather forecast prompted careful consideration of the passage ahead. The beginning of the week looked benign enough but from Wednesday onward the weather was forecast to deteriorate. I'd originally planned to visit Skye and Loch Harport but the Outer Hebrides lie on the far side of the Minches, a stretch of water that relishes its notoriety. If the weather was set to turn ugly the sooner we crossed the Minches the better, and once there the eastern coastline of the islands would shelter us from south-westerly winds, and enable us to complete the trip to Stornoway. Reluctantly I waved goodbye to another planned destination. The crew understood the logic and we shaped a course for Loch Boisdale on South Uist.

The gentle breeze and slight swell hardly confirmed the forecast of rough weather to come, but nobody complained as we reached across the South Minch. High overhead the first streaks of cirrus clouds hinted at the approaching depression, but that was for another day. An enormous freighter crossed our course and not long after, on the radio, we heard the watch keeper signing off with the coastguards having transited the controlled waters. Controlled waters because it wouldn't do for two of these huge vessels to come head to head among the islands. I felt a mounting sense of excitement as the smudge on the horizon steadily grew more defined. We really were entering the remote areas, with romantic names like Eriskay that I'd only heard before in travel documentaries. Near the tip of South Uist lies Loch Boisdale. The pilot book promised a few moorings and it remained to be seen whether any would be spare. If there were none we would have to anchor. A row of houses on the hills above the harbour revealed themselves to be disappointingly dull, more like military barracks. We picked up the last of the mooring buoys, tucked into a bay just round the headland from the large ferry quay. The dinghy was inflated and we headed for shore. There was a tourist information office where we discovered that the shops would be closing in ten minutes and the best showers were to be had in the hotel overlooking the harbour. We trotted into a general store.

'Good afternoon,' I said. 'Have you got any bread?'

'No,' came the reply.

'How about jam?'

'No.'

'Cake?'

'No.'

I looked quizzically at the figure behind the counter. My stare prompted his final offering, 'You best try the butchers round the corner. He might have more of what you want.'

It was now ten minutes before closing time. I ran down the street to where a seemingly rundown garage, but labelled 'Butcher', sold versions of most of what we needed. From there we walked into the hotel, a grand old pile, and asked about showers.

'Aye, no problem. Follow me.' The barman took us along a corridor to what looked like the staff quarters. We handed over a couple of pounds and washed away the salt. In the bar we sank into huge sofas, sipping pints, and admiring the stags' heads protruding from the walls, the fishing rods and shields gracing the beams.

'When we're back on the boat,' asked Geoff, 'where can I plug in my hair-dryer?'

I spluttered in my beer. 'Your what?'

Geoff looked hurt. 'My hairdryer. It is a travelling one.' I looked at Geoff's luxuriant head covering and reflected, for what would not be the last time on the trip, that those who still have it flaunt it, and relish its care. For those of us for whom eggshell finish is the norm, such pampering is irrelevant.

'Maybe when we get to the next marina we can find you a plug. For now you'll just have to shake and go.' Alan and Mike smirked and Geoff pulled a face. We drank up and retired to the boat, much cleaner, but with damp hair.

The next morning the forecast proved correct. Thick dark clouds scudded across the mooring, and a south westerly wind shook the rigging. We decided to head up the coast towards Loch Maddy on North Uist. According to the pilot the harbour offered good shelter, once you have negotiated the rock-strewn entrance. We nosed out into the Minch and turned northwards. *Shearwater* sped along on a broad reach, revelling in her fastest point of sailing. The wind blew off the mountains in bullying gusts, strengthening during the morning to the point where the boat began to round up, or slew round in the squalls as the rudder became overpowered.

'We need to put in a reef,' I shouted. Alan and Mike knew what was going on but Geoff looked blank. I went into a lengthy explanation of the procedure: tightening the topping lift to support the boom, freeing the main halyard, taking in the reef, then making fast the reefing line and re-tensioning the halyard, before finally freeing off the topping lift. Geoff stared at me.

'Ok, I've got all that—but why?' he said. I took a deep breath then realised that in my haste to concentrate on the process perhaps I'd not made clear why we were doing it.

'It's how we reduce the sail area, to reduce the pressure on the rig. If we don't the boat will be blown over on its ear and we'll all have more than just wet hair. Got it?'

Geoff nodded. I wasn't sure if he was just winding me up. Couldn't blame him really. Despite reefing, *Shearwater* was screaming along and in no time we could alter course towards the entrance. I ran through the course notes in preparation to navigate up the loch. It looked pretty tight, but of more concern at that moment was an ominous rain cloud heading our way. With about a mile to go we were hit by a vicious squall which flattened the surface of the sea and wiped out our visibility.

'We can't make our approach in this,' I shouted. 'Let's head out to sea again until it's cleared.' Alan put the helm over and we gybed, first heaving in the main sheet to prevent the boom crashing across the boat. The squall passed and we tacked back again when the entrance reappeared through the mist. It was a tense reach up the loch, with me glued to the plotter at the chart table and Mike shouting down the identity of the navigation marks as we sped by. We avoided the rocks and found a clear patch of water in which to round up and drop the sails before starting the engine. It had been an exciting sail. In a narrow spit of water close to the ferry terminal we made fast to a mooring, running our thickest rope through the heavy iron ring on top of the buoy.

By now a full gale was blowing. I doubled up the mooring warp in case one chafed through and retreated to the cabin. It was only thirty metres to the shore, but the strong wind and the absence of any sheltered quay persuaded us to put off any landing until the next morning. We had plenty of provisions and ate a good meal on board. Later in the evening a ferry rumbled alongside the quay, dwarfing us. It made fast and shut down the engines, staying put for the night. The activities of the day, a full stomach and some whisky tasting induced an agreeable drowsiness and we succumbed to it early, hoping the weather would improve overnight.

The next morning my alarm sounded and I groped for the phone. There was a good internet signal and the inshore forecast flickered onto the screen. It didn't make good reading, as confirmed by the rain drumming on the fore-hatch. In the strong wind *Shearwater* was yawing from side to side on her mooring. I went back to sleep. Eventually over breakfast we reviewed our plans.

'Stornoway is about 50 miles away and there are three days left. We could split the passage at Loch Tarbert but that involves a long approach to a safe anchorage and if the weather proves uncooperative we might get stuck there.' I suggested we stayed put for the day and then, if the weather improved the next day, we would head straight for Stornoway, giving us a day in hand if we needed to seek shelter on route. No one had a better plan.

Geoff looked a bit pale and said he'd had a torrid night. He'd woken up to use the heads, (the nautical name for a toilet). He'd sat down to discover the water level in the bowl had risen to the point where it met his undercarriage. He'd shot up again banging his head on the ceiling and, declining to trouble me, had retired to his bunk having forgotten what he'd got up for in the first place.

Once again the dinghy was inflated. The rain reduced to a dull drizzle and I ferried the crew ashore one at a time. We lifted the dinghy and outboard engine up a narrow set of steps to a secure place well above sea level. After thirty six hours on board it was good to stretch our legs. Loch Maddy didn't offer much apart from a ferry quay, a tourist information office and a few cottages either side of the pub. Alan and I bought some Harris Tweed caps, and then we found the local community centre and sipped coffee while another heavy rain shower passed through.

A fish van drew up and we joined the queue of locals to buy some superb scallops and a thick piece of cod. There was enough to feed four of us, all for twenty
pounds. We found the local grocery, which was well stocked, and by then the lure
of the hotel with hot showers and a pint of beer proved irresistible. We knew the
routine now, but there was only one shower available for visiting yachtsmen and
another yacht's crew were in line before us. When I eventually got my shower
we'd had lunch and two pints apiece. Before re-launching the dinghy I produced
two foldable water containers and we took 20 litres of fresh water back to the boat
and topped up *Shearwater*'s tank.

It was still blowing hard the next morning when we slipped the mooring. I
reckoned on a fast passage up to Stornoway, the only concern being the sea state.
The gale had whipped up the waves, which on our course up the coast would
produce a following sea. This is always uncomfortable for a small yacht because
the rollers pick up the back of the boat causing it to wallow from side to side. Sure
enough, as we cleared the cliffs at the entrance to the loch *Shearwater*'s motion
became uneasy. Geoff soon looked uncomfortable, turning white. He said he was
going below to use the heads. I realised he wouldn't be re-appearing and for the
rest of the passage lay in his bunk with a bucket for company.

I set two reefs in the mainsail and rigged a preventer. This is a rope attached
to the outer end of the mainsail boom and tied down forward. If the boat gybes
unintentionally a preventer stops the boom from crashing across the boat. Most
sailing fatalities are caused by someone being struck on the head by a boom. In
this fashion we roared up the coast, past the Sound of Scalpay and the Shiant
isles. The islands looked worth a visit on a calm day but thunderous dark clouds
rolled over us from behind the mountains of Harris and the sea was ugly. Along
the rugged coastline occasionally we could make out the odd crofter's cottage. It
beggared belief that people would choose such a desolate place to live.

Alan was on the helm when Mike shouted to me, 'There's a pump running
in the cabin.' I hopped below, and heard the fresh water pump going flat out. No
taps were running and this noise usually signals the fresh water tank has run empty. But how could that be when we'd shipped twenty litres on board, the night before? I heard a sloshing below the cabin sole and looked down to see water washing over the floor boards. We'd lost our entire fresh water supply. I sighed. It was

just as well we were heading for a decent sized harbour, because the unknown cause of the leak was a worry. If the water tank itself was leaking, it was a stainless tank set under the cockpit and almost impossible to get at.

There was enough bottled water to make a brew. I rustled up a hot meal, sparing Geoff, who was sound asleep. A heavy rain shower engulfed us and then the wind eased. I shook out the reefs, anxious to maintain speed and get tucked up in Stornoway before the forecast big blow arrived. We passed the entrance to Loch Tarbert and from then on along this wild coast there was no more shelter before Stornoway. The wind was backing steadily throughout the day. What had started out as a south westerly was now due south. I goose-winged the genoa, setting it on the opposite side of the mast to the mainsail. *Shearwater* could smell a safe harbour and romped along. The lighthouse at Arnish Point hove into view. We gybed the genoa back and hardened up for the approach to the harbour. Well inside the estuary there was enough room to turn up into the wind and furl the mainsail. I reported our arrival to the coastguards who complimented us on our arrival, spot on the estimated time. Praise indeed. A mass of rhododendron bushes painted the shoreline a deep pink.

I called the harbour authority and requested a berth for four nights, enough time to change crew and wait for the weather to settle. I made the call in some trepidation as the pilot book suggested that spaces were few and far between, but we were in luck and they directed us to a berth where the harbourmaster met us. As we motored past the fishermen's quay we had to dodge a huge seal drifting around the unloading vessels, begging for his supper. The harbourmaster was standing on a short stretch of pontoon between two other moored craft. A strong wind was blowing off the pontoon and we had some fun getting alongside, aborting our first approach, but got a bow line ashore at the second attempt. The burly officer heaved in our stern line as easily as if we were a small dinghy. We moored opposite the imposing Lews Castle. Some buildings of character at last, I thought.

'Welcome to Stornoway,' he said. We had arrived. Mission accomplished for the week.

I went ashore to complete some paperwork in the harbourmaster's office and to check out the shower facilities, leaving the crew to investigate the source of the fresh water leak. On the way I spotted a large bosun's store and what looked like a decent fish restaurant where I booked us a table. Back on *Shearwater*, I was met by Alan, who announced they'd found a water hose had become detached under the sink. The little darlings had already fixed it and were busy refilling the water tank.

My gamble on the fish restaurant paid off and we enjoyed what was now becoming a weekly ritual, savouring good food and wine while reminiscing on the highs and lows of the week. I was forgiven for my sharp rebukes over seamanship sins, and I made light of the howlers. We retired to *Shearwater* for a wee dram and the precursor to a blissful night's kip.

The next day was Friday, a whole day to spend luxuriously exploring Stornoway. We enjoyed a leisurely breakfast and walked up into town. I lugged a large sack containing two weeks of laundry and dumped them on the counter of a shop that promised a same day turnaround. The lass behind the counter didn't react too violently to both the size and sniff of my bag and I beat a hasty retreat before she could change her mind over the price. We sipped coffee in a café, provisioned up for the following week, and the crew went to buy their tickets for the ferry crossing to Ullapool and combined coach ticket to Fort William. Geoff came back with his tail between his legs because Alan and Mike bought the last two 'old gits' concessions.

After lunch we walked around the head of the harbour into the graceful parkland which is the setting for of Lews Castle. I wasn't sure whether someone just missed out one of the letters in Lewis or whether the spelling of its name had been deliberate. An ongoing refurbishment denied us a look around. It was built relatively recently in 1847 by Sir John Matheson, who made his fortune from the Chinese opium trade. Who thought drug barons were a recent phenomenon? He was succeeded in 1915 by Lord Leverhulme, who established the much more respectable Lever Bros, later Unilever. In semi retirement he bought the island and was a philanthropist who set out to establish a fish-canning industry centred in Stornoway. His plan had been to relieve the extreme poverty that pervaded the place, but after toiling for many years the poor chap died, his efforts in vain, as the suspicious population rejected his help.

In the evening we had a couple of beers in the hotel restaurant opposite the pontoons, woofing down a bowl of chips which we took to be complimentary but apparently had been intended for another table. The longest day of the year ended in damp drizzle, the town ghostly empty. We ate on board. Alan prepared his signature dish of stuffed, baked peppers and was forgiven for writing off the dinner plates which, although oven proof, objected to being dangled over the flames. I put on a disc of favourite operatic arias which prompted a heated discussion with Geoff as to whether or not opera is pretentious. Mike attempted mediation and Alan kept his head down preparing the meal, no doubt thinking what an opinionated lot these villagers can be. Good food and wine administered cooling balm and we bedded down good pals as ever.

We were up early on the Saturday. It was still drizzling so I waved the lads off from the boat and took a shower, spurning the chance of a lie in—it seemed a waste of what I had come to savour, a day to myself. My crew for the next week were due to arrive on the evening ferry from Ullapool. I needed to replace a gas cylinder and lugged the heavy canister through an industrial estate to a builder's yard where I was met by a fierce looking lad. As he took my credit card I noticed his bandaged knuckles and couldn't imagine how he'd incurred those. After placing my card in the machine, he paused and took out of his pocket a mobile phone and began typing. It was only back on the boat that I thought 'what have I just done?' I was convinced I'd been the naive victim of a card fraud and rushed back up into town, armed with my iPad. The library offered Wi-Fi and I needed to update my blog but more importantly I wanted to check my bank account, certain I would already find it cleaned out of funds. Needless to say my scepticism was groundless.

Ten

و

A S I WANDERED BACK THROUGH TOWN I was struck by the faces of the Stornoway women. Many of them showed their Nordic genes, striking blonde hair and moon shaped eyes. On the quayside a magnificent cast statue of some fisher folk paid tribute to the town's historical links with herring fishing. I bought some boat bits in the chandlers, mooched around a craft fair searching for a birthday present for Jan, then back on board cooked my first meal using one of Rick Stein's fish recipes. I'd originally dreamed we would be catching our supper most days but had failed miserably to date, and the mackerel came courtesy of an angler returning to the quay side with a box full of fish. He offered me some and I humbly accepted three, conscious of the seal still patrolling the harbour. The poor creature couldn't access Tesco, and here I was taking three fresh beauties that he would have devoured in an instant. Needless to say lunch was delicious.

My brother Paul phoned to say they would be arriving on the ferry at 2100. I walked to the hotel and they agreed to hold a table for dinner. The rain became a steady drizzle and I rigged the cockpit tent, pleased to find my patch repairs in Cardiff had cured most of the leaks. A guy from another boat called by, intrigued to know what class *Shearwater* was. My new twin spreader mast deceives most people. He and his partner were doing the trip anticlockwise. They'd sailed from Orkney directly to Stornoway. We exchanged tips about harbours and passages. Re-telling the worse bits is always as enjoyable as recalling the best. The drizzle continued and in the early evening I heard the sound of a pipe band performing in the square at the end of the harbour. By the time I walked up to meet the ferry they had disappeared and just a damp mist draped the heavy granite buildings. It was hard to conceive being anywhere where it would feel less like a midsummer's evening.

The ferry docked and amongst the disembarking hoards I made out the familiar shapes of my brother Paul, the somewhat taller figure of my brother-in-law Bob, and Steve from Ogston whom I'd only met a couple of times before. Ironically, because of the length of their journey Paul and Bob already knew Steve better than I did. I helped carry their kit back to the boat and we retreated quickly to the hotel where the bar staff were anxiously awaiting our order. Over dinner I set out the plans for the next few days. This would be the week that had most occupied my thoughts when planning the trip and since setting out: the rounding of Cape Wrath and the passage to Stromness in Orkney.

'The forecast is dire. Unless there's a distinct improvement overnight we won't be going anywhere tomorrow.' Back on board they sorted out their bunks and stowed gear. 'No rush in the morning, chaps,' I said as we turned in.

Just after six the next day I was awoken by the sound of IT bells and whistles. I was becoming accustomed to the various smart phone and tablet gadgets each crew brought along and resolved early on to say nothing unless they went off all night. I made only one rule, to ban taking mobile calls when we were sailing. I could just imagine someone having to take a call in the middle of some tricky manoeuvre. Eventually the cacophony of beeps and trills roused me from my snooze and I got up to investigate. Steve and Bob were sat on their bunks, fully dressed, looking like naughty boys who'd opened their Christmas presents as soon as Santa had left the room.

'What's up?' I said.' It's only 6.30. Can't you hear the wind out there? I said we'd be going nowhere today. Have a lie in.' They looked a bit chastened and I retired for another hour. Things were a bit muted over breakfast. Suddenly there was a commotion in the harbour. I looked across to where the lifeboat was stationed and saw the crew running down the gangway. The engines roared into action. We then witnessed what must be one of the shortest rescues on record. The boat left its mooring and motored sedately for fifty metres across to the other side of the inner harbour where a Dutch yacht was beginning to heel over. It must have cut the corner on its approach to the pontoons and caught the edge of the rocks. The lifeboat soon got a heavy warp on board and dragged the yacht clear, before towing it to a vacant berth. It was all over in less than thirty minutes.

The forecast confirmed my suspicion. It was not the weather for crossing the top of the Minch.

'Right, no sailing today. Who fancies exploring Lewis? We could hire a car?'

We all agreed and I rang the car-hire number on the information sheet the harbourmaster had supplied. A woman with a strong Highland accent answered.

'Well it's closed today being Sunday but I could come in to the office if you want,' she trilled.

'If you don't mind that would be fine,' I said. 'Shall we say ten o'clock?'

At the appointed hour we stood outside what was marked on the map as the car hire office. It looked more like a charity shop. A succession of cars drove slowly past, their occupants in Sunday best glaring at us. We weren't sure whether they felt we should also be making our way to church or whether we looked like vagrants about to break in. We realised the map was out of date and finally located the office.

'Is there anywhere in particular you would recommend heading for?' I asked.

'Well no, not really. You see today is Sunday.'

'Yes.'

'So you see everything will be closed.'

'What, even the tourist attractions, the art galleries, potteries, crofters cottages, that sort of thing?'

'Yes, I'm afraid so.'

I sighed. 'What about restaurants and cafes? Will we be able get any lunch anywhere?' She shook her head. 'A sandwich?' I pleaded.

'Well there is a petrol station on the outskirts of the town. I believe you might get a sandwich there.'

We drove off to find the garage and gratefully scooped up the last few ham rolls. On the way we passed the supermarket.

'Blimey,' said Paul, 'even Tesco's closed.'

Driving around the island the only signs of life were in the car parks for the many chapels, which were all rammed full. We found a couple of sites of Neolithic standing stones which presumably the church elders had found it impracticable to close, or perhaps they were just dismissive of the religion once practised there. We stood next to the lighthouse on Tiumpan Head, struggling to stay on our feet in the strong wind. Looking out over the boiling, cold grey seas of the North Minch we could see a fishing boat battling to make progress. At Point of

Ness we sat in the car eating our lunch watching huge waves testing the strength of the stone harbour. It was evident that often the sea won the contest; under the foaming breakers the outer end of the harbour lay in a heap of rubble. Gannets performed aerial acrobatics, gliding gently above us before diving at breakneck speed to plummet into the sea. Steve captured one on his camera just at the moment the bird entered the water, legs and wings tightly stretched out behind.

By mid afternoon we had driven to the western shore of the island. We found a traditional crofter's cottage, low with a peat roof. It would have been fascinating to look around, but was closed. We stumbled upon a hotel and restaurant and tentatively parked up. I went in.

'Hi, I know you're closed for lunch,' I said,' But wondered if there was any chance of a cup of tea?'

The young guy paused and replied, 'Well I suppose we could do that.'

Encouraged I added, 'And possibly any cake?' There was another pause and he said, 'I'll go and check in the kitchen.'

I called in the lads and we sat at a table and waited. Eventually he re-appeared bearing a teapot and cups and some portions of cherry cake, each individually wrapped. Steve recognised them from the hospitality trays in hotel rooms. I questioned the waiter on the Sunday closing thing.

'Are there any statutory restrictions?'

'No, not that I know of. It's just that Lewis is firmly in the grip of the Church. Whenever anyone tries to open anything on a Sunday there's uproar. It was only last year that CalMac began ferry services on a Sunday and then the first few ships were met with hostile banner waving.'

We did one last set of standing stones, this one important enough to justify an information centre, which was closed of course, and decided we'd had enough. We drove back to Stornoway as the dismal day drew to a close. At least the restaurant in the harbour hotel put on a decent evening meal so we didn't starve. Back on *Shearwater* I said, 'I'll check the weather at about seven and we'll make a decision then. Night all.'

At six the next morning I was awoken by a loud series of beeps and a bustle which seemed to emanate from Steve's bunk. I groaned. I've got a serious authority problem here, I thought. The noise continued for a few minutes, causing me to poke my head out of my cabin. Steve was again up and dressed, bunk cleared away. Bob was still in his bunk. 'I told him, Skipper,' said Bob.

'Sorry,' said Steve. 'I mis-read the clock.'

Again I retired to my bunk. When I did re-surface to check the forecast it looked hopeful. A fresh but not dangerous westerly should speed us across to the mainland to Kinlochbervie. We could miss out Loch Inver and that would place us just thirty miles down the coast from Cape Wrath. We motored over to the re-fuelling berth and I clambered up the tall quayside and went to pay the harbour dues while the crew topped up the diesel tank. Despite the Sunday closing and drab weather there was a great spirit in Stornoway and a quality to its buildings that had been sadly lacking elsewhere on the Outer Hebrides. I waved a fond farewell and braced myself for the biggest challenge of the trip.

Despite the gale the day before the sea proved to be smooth. Paul and Steve soon got into the sailing. They also began vying with each other for the best photographs of the seals and dolphins accompanying us, along with the puffins and guillemots. Bob looked apprehensive as we sailed out of sight of land. I set the mainsail with a single reef and *Shearwater* scooted over the waves. The wind was in a good quarter for sailing and we could hold a straight line course towards our destination. By the end of the afternoon the tall mountains on the mainland rose clear above the clouds, the wind eased and I shook out the reef. Bob relaxed. He hadn't sailed as much as the other guys and probably felt a bit daunted at his first passage across a notoriously tricky stretch of water, not that I'd made much of it so far. It seemed better to talk up a passage when you re-lived it over a pint.

Kinlochbervie is literally 'the smaller loch off Loch Bervie.' The entrance to the main loch nestles between tall rock faces and is impossible to see until you're close in to shore. Once again we had to put our trust in the instruments. Half a mile off we stowed the sails and turned on the engine. I sat in the cockpit nursing the iPad which faithfully showed our track towards the gap; Steve held a true course and Paul and Bob scanned the shore with binoculars. A fishing boat overtook us and made life easy, revealing the course for the final approach. We passed close by the sheer face of the cliffs on the port side as we entered the loch, which was bathed in the golden rays of the setting sun. Tall beacons marked each side of the entrance to Kinlochbervie harbour and at the visitors' pontoon we squeezed in a gap between a Moody 38 from Croabhaven, and Lindisfarne, a pretty single hander whose skipper was most appreciative of our seamanship which left intact the self steering gear hung off his transom. They were very friendly and anxious to hear about our crossing, having been weather-bound in the harbour for several days.

Despite it being nine-thirty, it was still daylight. As we made secure the harbourmaster strode down the gangway and welcomed us. I wondered if these guys ever went off duty. I paid for a night. He confirmed my thoughts that the forecast the next morning looked good for rounding the Cape and that slack water was the best time for the passage. Paul made dinner, and I checked the tides. Slack water off Cape Wrath would be at seven thirty the next morning. We needed at least three hours to sail up the coast, probably having to motor as I didn't expect any wind first thing. It meant an early start so we turned in after eating.

'Shame we're getting up so early, you won't have any use for this,' I said to Steve holding up a 'post it' sticker on which I'd drawn some clock hands showing seven o'clock and the inscription 'Steve's getting up time.' He saw the funny side of it, I think.

We arose at first light just after four. A mist hung over the loch. During the night I was woken by an enormous deep sea trawler grumbling seawards. The receding tide had left the entrance to the harbour as a narrow gap between the rocks, but it was well buoyed. We turned to starboard and set a course outside the rocky island of Dubh Sgeir (Sgeir being Gaelic for Skerry, our old friend meaning rock), presided over by a sturdy-looking lighthouse. On rounding the island we altered direction to keep as close inshore as seemed comfortable because we were punching the last of the ebb tide which scurries down the coast at this point. The tall mountains to the East put on a spectacular show. Clouds rolled off the summits, engulfed in red flames which we hoped was normal and didn't portend bad weather.

We made good progress and when we were a few miles off the Cape I set a course to place us one and half miles off the headland for our rounding. I picked up the early morning inshore forecast which confirmed that of the previous evening—still fair with a forecast calm sea. I felt a tingle of excitement that we were on track to round the 'big one' at our first attempt. I wondered what the nautical equivalent was for 'don't count your chickens before they're hatched.'

All eyes were on the tall, bluff, cliff face jutting defiantly out into the sea. I kept checking our course on the chart plotter, anxious to detect early any strong currents setting us towards the rocks. Despite the relatively calm day, and that we had arrived almost dead on predicted slack water, the seas were incredibly confused. Waves rolled in from all directions to converge at this point. We could see flashes of white from the breakers crashing at the foot of the cliffs. It didn't bear thinking about to imagine what it would be like trying to round the Cape in any other conditions.

Slowly the headland altered shape, the north coast opened up and our charted position entitled me to make the log entry I had been imagining for a long time: '0730—rounded Cape Wrath.' Ok it wasn't exactly Cape Horn but in our little boat, at this moment, it might just as well have been. We all grinned in relief as *Shearwater* eased her course to head north-east towards Orkney.

With the kettle on the stove I sat at the chart table considering our options for the remainder of the passage. As the pilot book says, 'The north coast of Scotland is not a place for the faint hearted or the inexperienced.' Along the sixty miles of rocky coastline between Cape Wrath and Duncansby Head there is just one deep water harbour, and a couple of lochs offering safe anchorages—if the wind is not in the wrong direction. One of these is named Loch Eriboll, but during the Second World War the navy christened it Loch Horrible on account of the poor shelter it afforded the convoy escort vessels. The only deep water harbour, tucked in to the west of John o' Groats, is Scrabster, the ferry port serving Orkney. This had been the original destination when we set off that morning. From there it is only a thirty mile crossing to Stromness, our final destination for the week. But that would mean another day's sailing. From the pilot it didn't look as though Scrabster held any particular interest. I worked up some calculations and took coffee up to the cockpit.

'We have another option, chaps. We have the day ahead of us. From here it's forty-five miles to Scrabster, but only a further eight to Stromness. If we were to arrive there this evening that would give us two clear days to explore ashore and still catch the ferry back to the mainland on Friday morning.'

There was a general nod of approval so I continued. 'According to the pilot the currents in Hoy Sound are fearsome and today we are at the top of springs.

It's important to arrive there at slack water which for us today means 1800. To arrive at the right time we need to get close enough to Orkney to be able to punch the last of the tide and yet not arrive too early.' We decided to go for it and during the day had the unusual experience of finely adjusting our boat speed. I monitored progress each hour. Normally we would just plough on regardless and hope for a quick passage. When the tide was with us we could afford to allow what gentle breeze there was to waft us along, using the engine to adjust our speed as the tide turned foul.

It was a delightful day. Paul and Steve, the 'paps,' competed for the best bird life shot, snapping the gannets diving and the puffins dancing in the waves. The sun shone and we relaxed, soaking in the special feel of the place. We had to pinch ourselves to believe that Cape Wrath had surrendered so meekly and that now we were cruising along the north coast of Scotland as though it was the Devon Riviera. In the afternoon the outline of Hoy, the tallest of the Orkney islands, began to grow on the horizon. We studied the course of the ferries crossing from Scrabster trying to work out exactly where the entrance to the sound lay. The Old Man of Hoy, a tall stack of rock on the south western tip of Hoy, became distinct from the mainland.

We were focused on picking out the buoys marking the approach to the Sound, when a strange wheezing noise on our port side caught our attention. An orca whale was blowing air; its shiny black back arched gracefully just metres from the boat, before gliding back beneath the waves. It was a magical moment sealing a memorable day. But we weren't quite finished. On entering the Sound, although it was slack water, eddies of current swirled on either side revealing the turbulence that would wreak havoc when the tide flowed back into Scapa Flow. It was exciting just to be mouthing these evocative place names.

We furled the sails and slowly motored up the approach channel to Stromness harbour. Lining the western edge of the harbour stood delightful stone cottages, each commanding its own quayside. Interspersed amongst them were huge gantries linked, no doubt, to servicing the nearby oil terminal on the Island of Flotta in Scapa Flow. The yacht berths were pontoons tucked behind the fishing quay at the head of the harbour. There were plenty of spaces and we tied up, soon to be met by Bobbie Moore, a retired baker and one of the volunteers who run the

marina. He was a lovely guy who warmly welcomed us and talked through the facilities. I planned to leave *Shearwater* for a few days and felt she would be in good
hands. I sighed contentedly. We had arrived at the top of the course.

If it's possible to sleep all night with a grin on your face that was me. We had
reached the most northerly part of the voyage on time and had escaped Cape
Wrath. The following morning we met up with the crew of Lindisfarne, one of
the yachts we'd moored next to in Kinlochbervie. They'd left after us and had en-
dured some lumpy conditions off the Cape. There was another yacht in the harbour which had taken our course a few days earlier and had frightened themselves
silly. On the pontoon I recognised the red hull of Rival, and the couple I'd met at
Holyhead, which now seemed a lifetime ago. They'd already spent a few days on
the island and told us not to miss a visit to Skara Brae.

'What's that?' I said, advertising my ignorance.

'You know,' she said. 'The Neolithic village settlement that was uncovered
when a huge storm washed away the sand dunes.'

'Oh, yes of course,' I lied. 'Is it good?'

'It's fantastic,' she said before coming closer to whisper. 'Back in Holyhead,
after you'd gone home we couldn't help noticing that you've got the shackle on
your anchor attached to the wrong part. If the tide changes we think you could
drag your anchor.' I mumbled something and retired to the boat feeling a cross
between embarrassed and irritated. The anchor was designed to have a sliding
shackle or a fixed attachment point enabling you to clear the anchor if it becomes
jammed under rocks. I'd thought about which attachment point to use and con-
cluded that you could never know when the anchor might foul the bottom so
you'd be better off having it on the sliding point all the time. And then along came
someone who appeared to be more intrepid and therefore obviously more experienced who suggested the contrary and raised a doubt in my mind. Perhaps I'll
change the fixing when no one's looking, I thought.

We had a whole day free to explore. The suggestion to visit Skara Brae didn't
need further consideration and so, wearing appropriate summer gear—long trousers, shirt, jumper and anorak—we jumped on a bus taking a tourist route to Kirkwall, via the archaeological site and the major standing stones. We were fascinated
by Skara Brae. The stone buildings have been painstakingly uncovered and are re-

markably intact given that they date from around 3000BC, five hundred years or more prior to the dynasty which built the pyramids. The bus stopped long enough for a visit and then took us to the standing stones. There's never much information at these sites, probably because it would all be complete guesswork. No one can be certain why such huge structures were put in place, but they never cease to impress. It began to rain and we re-boarded the bus and meandered along winding lanes amid soft rolling countryside, more like Dorset than the wilds of northern Britain, and far more inviting than the Outer Hebrides. I felt Jan would have loved it although the chances of my prising her away from the garden seemed remote.

The bus deposited us in Kirkwall, the other main town on the largest island, known as Mainland. We sampled the local beer and for lunch tried the unlikely combination of black pudding with scallops. It was delicious. We pottered amongst the craft shops buying trinkets for loved ones. Paul bought some superb Argyll steak, not for a loved one but the next best thing, his crew mates. Back in Stromness we walked the narrow streets, soaking up the history. The museum offered a great exhibition, charting the strong trading links between the town and the Hudson's Bay Trading Company in Canada. It turns out that Stromness is on the same latitude as Hudson's Bay. No doubt it was convenient for the supply ships to be able to sail due west and return with furs and whatever else the company was selling. Photographs and paintings showed the tiny wharves in the harbour teeming with sailing ships of all descriptions.

The town was a breeding ground for intrepid explorers. Many of the houses wore blue plaques depicting the history of former residents. I was particularly taken with one occupied by Eliza Fraser, who set off from Stromness for Australia and was shipwrecked off Queensland in 1836 and captured by Aborigines. She spent many years understanding their culture and gave her name to the largest sand island in the world, near Brisbane. Jan and I went there on the first visit to see our eldest son who happens to be called Fraser. The coincidence tickled me enough to send him a text about it.

We had a pre-dinner pint in the *Ferry Boat Inn* near the quayside and Paul worked his magic with the steak. I enjoyed yet another great meal on *Shearwater*. The crew had bonded well. Even Steve managed a good night's sleep. On Thursday we re-fuelled and set off for a day sail in Scapa Flow. Having arrived early in the week I was keen not to short change the crew and suggested a day out. By leaving in the morning and returning before tea time we could avoid the current.

We motored out of the harbour and almost immediately encountered strong overfalls which tossed the boat around. Under full power we escaped their clutches. The tide was still running strongly into Scapa Flow. I studied the chart and was concerned by a long thin obstruction showing as extending across the Sound. I couldn't work out how much depth we had over it and caused a small panic by deciding we'd have to round the end. Paul was on the helm and had to practically head back towards Stromness to counteract the tide and clear the outer marker buoy.

A fresh wind blew across Scapa Flow. We reefed the sails and Bob took the helm for a lively sail. There proved to be no time to anchor for lunch before the ebb got under way and we had to head back. As we approached the entrance to Stromness, looking towards the sound we could see a line of broken sea where the overfalls were flexing their muscles. On the way back we followed a fishing boat which must have drawn more water than us. He steamed straight over the obstruction I'd panicked about in the morning. It turned out to be one of the Churchill breakwaters constructed during the Second World War. They were built to prevent German submarines from entering the enclosed stretch of water that was used for the assembly of convoys and their naval escort vessels bound for Murmansk. According to the locals the breakwaters have altered the tidal flows between the islands.

Back in harbour we enjoyed some evening sun; it was even warm enough to sit in the cockpit with a pre-dinner drink before we headed off into town to a restaurant Steve had spotted. We were up early to clean the boat and pack. I joined the crew for the return journey home. This comprised a ferry crossing to Scrabster, coach to Inverness and then by car to Winster. We arrived fourteen hours later, a measure of how far I'd sailed.

Eleven

❦

A WEEK OF RURAL ENGLISH COUNTRY LIFE was to follow. After a brief sojourn in the summer warmth of my village it was time to continue the voyage. I flew back, changing flights at Inverness where I used the few hours between planes to visit the Culloden battlefield. On my last visit many years before, the site merely comprised a few notice boards and the re-constructed cottage. The cottage is still there but now alongside it sits a magnificent visitor centre, explaining all the history surrounding the massacre. I read about Bonnie Prince Charlie calling a meeting of the clan chieftains at Glen Finan. I read that his army had invaded England, making speedy progress down as far as Ashbourne, a stone's throw from my home village. At this point the chiefs refused his urging to continue to London and they returned to Scotland where they would be massacred by troops under the command of the Duke of Cumberland. Over fifteen hundred Scots were slaughtered in the battle with just fifty English deaths. I realised that being fortunate enough to visit so much of our islands in one trip provided the opportunity to link up much of its history.

I caught a taxi back to the airport to board the light aircraft which runs to Orkney and then on up to Shetland. There were only twelve seats, mostly occupied by tough looking oil rig workers. I sat next to pretty lass who was up from London, visiting friends. She was more impressed with my adventure than I suspected the guys would have been. At Kirkwall airport it was down to earth in more ways than one. The plane and bus timetables didn't match up and I had a choice between waiting for over an hour and paying handsomely for a taxi. I was keen to see *Shearwater* again so shelled out. The boat was waiting patiently on the visitor's pontoons. I ate on board and slept well, stirred occasionally by the wind raking the harbour. The next morning it was sunny but a cold wind pierced the cockpit. I was grateful that most of my jobs were 'indoors.' I changed the engine oil and tightened up some bolts on the rudder stock. Dave sent me a text to announce his arrival on the two-thirty ferry and soon enough he was waving down from the quayside. It was good to have him on board again where I regaled him with our adventures since he left the boat in Holyhead. He said the crews he'd met at Ogston had all been full of their experiences, which was pleasing. I'd have hated to think they'd suffered in silence.

Syd was due to arrive on the evening ferry. I suggested to Dave he should visit the museum while I finished the maintenance. We met up in the *Ferry Boat* and supped a pint whilst watching the tennis players sweat it out in the fierce sun at Wimbledon. It was hard to believe we were in the same islands. We postponed dinner, hanging on for Syd, who in true seaman's fashion rolled up with a kit bag over his shoulder. He'd already eaten so he watched Dave and me tuck in whilst sampling the beer. I'd not been too precise on the date of my return to the boat so Syd had booked to stay overnight in the pub. He joined us on board early the next morning. The weather looked fair for a passage to Longhope on Hoy, from where we could plot our escape back to the mainland and begin the big dash south. I'd planned to get down to London in two weeks, which was somewhat ambitious. I'd read that on the East coast safe harbours were few and far between, and wanted to make as much progress as the weather would permit.

Bobbie came down to the pontoon and apologetically gave me the bill for the stay. It was no surprise and I thanked him for his assistance. As he left another older guy called over, 'Have you seen anyone on that boat? I'm looking for Sean?' He pointed out a rugged looking cruising yacht moored a few berths along. He continued, 'We're off round to Longhope this morning, for the regatta.' My ears picked up. So far on the trip I seemed to have arrived too early or too late to catch any local events.

'There was someone on board earlier this morning,' I said.

'We're taking the yoles round there for the racing.'

I'd noticed these lovely looking craft in the harbour. Flat bottomed, clinker planking with a gunter rig. The enquirer introduced himself. 'I'm Bill, the chairman of the Orkney Yole Association.'

'They're great looking boats, I'd love to have a sail in one,' I said. 'We're heading for Longhope this morning. Perhaps we'll see you there.'

'Oh, aye. We'll be along there,' he said. 'We might be able to get you a sail.' At that moment Sean turned up and Bill seemed relieved.

'OK, see you there,' I shouted as we cast off.

There was a fresh south-easterly wind whipping up the waves as we headed out across Scapa Flow. We reefed the main and put a couple of rolls in the genoa, and *Shearwater* bent to her task, beating energetically across the sound. As always the tide is everything and a strong flood in our favour made every tack worthwhile. We made great progress, outpacing Sean who was under power but towing two yoles astern. At the end of the sound we saw two other yoles which had set out under outboard engines. One had taken a heavy wave and was now under tow back to Stromness. I wondered whether we should have offered a tow but doubted whether our engine would have been powerful enough for the job. They were in no danger but sadly would miss out on the regatta.

It proved to be one of the best passages of the cruise. In the flat sheltered seas of Scapa Flow with a fresh breeze *Shearwater* was in her element. We zig-zagged between the islands, standing in as close as we dared, even managing to beat down Gutter Sound, a narrow inlet separating Rysa Little and Fara. We sailed numerous short tacks standing in close to the shore before at the last minute spinning *Shearwater* about to head back to the other side. We were well and truly warm by the time we could finally free off to cream up the Sound of Long Hope. I called the harbourmaster who said he could find us room inside the tiny harbour. As we approached the entrance, we could see the harbour was really no more than a ferry quay extension to an old stone wharf. Numerous racing dinghies criss-crossed the water giving a strangely busy feel to the isolated hamlet. On the grassy embankment alongside the pub a marquee had been erected with bunting flapping furiously in the breeze. We tucked into the harbour, rounding up alongside the fishing quay. A shiny lifeboat sat on its mooring pontoon. We edged alongside the stone wall and Dave jumped onto the steps to take our mooring lines up to some rusty iron rings. He found a couple of large fenders made from huge tractor tyres slung on ropes which we dangled over the edge to keep us off the barnacle-encrusted wall.

As soon as we moored Syd announced he was off to check out the beer. As much as anything he was itching to light up his pipe, which he soon had smoking, the rich aroma trailing behind him as he strode off up the hill. Bill appeared over the harbour wall.

'Are you wanting a sail in a yole?' he shouted down. We nodded eagerly.

'Well there's a race in about half an hour if you'd like to join us.'

'That'd be great,' I said. 'We'll be up with you shortly.'

We snatched a sandwich and put on our oilskins. The wind had dropped and a steady drizzle niggled us intermittently. Syd returned from the pub, pronounced the beer to be drinkable and said he wasn't one for racing and would watch from the quayside. Dave and I paid our entry fee and stood alongside Bill and Sean.

'There's just the one race,' said Bill. 'We don't race ourselves much.'

'That's no problem,' I said. 'Dave and I race a fair bit, although we've never sailed a yole.'

'Oh, that's grand,' said Bill. 'You can helm and we'll just crew.' It was getting better all the time, I thought.

We clambered down the harbour wall and over a fishing boat, negotiating the gnarled and rusty fishing gear. The yole was tied on the outside. We hoisted the sails and cast off. There was just enough breeze to edge out into the Sound. Bill said we would be racing in our own class with single and twin masted yoles, each having their own finish. In yacht racing the trick is to be crossing the start line exactly when the gun sounds. Too early and you have to re-start, too late and you begin at a disadvantage.

The warning signals were unsophisticated, white sticks held up on the quayside. We crept towards the start line, anxious to display our racing prowess. As the start gun fired the breeze lost its battle with the ebbing tide and we were nowhere near the line. Fortunately none of the other boats were either. For a few minutes it looked as though we'd never cross it but the wind rallied and we slowly got the craft moving, tacking up the sound in the wake of our main rival. Bill announced this boat was helmed by Angus, the sailing club commodore and coxswain of the lifeboat.

Angus rounded the windward mark about fifty metres ahead of us. We reached slowly across the sound to round the next mark closer to but still behind Angus.

'I've brought with me the trophy we won last year. I'm anxious to keep hold of it,' said Bill. Dave raised his eyebrows. No pressure there then, I thought. On the downwind leg we eased the mainsail sheet, allowing the long boom to swing out across the boat. I got Dave to hold the jib out on the other side, goose winging the rig. Angus looked back and copied our action. He had his family and dog on board. Dave loves dogs and called out to enquire the dog's name.

'Oscar,' came the reply.

Dave then began gently calling the dog's name, reasoning that if he could coax the canine out of the boat we might stand a chance. Oscar was too smart for that trick. However, using techniques honed on windless Wednesday nights at Ogston reservoir, we positioned our boat dead upwind of Angus and contrived to blanket his wind. He tried to steer out of our path but we stuck to his wake and slowly began to overhaul him. It's great to see the helm of a yacht looking anxiously back over his shoulder and then start to adjust all his sail controls. As we approached the downwind mark, we had crept inside Angus and were able to round ahead of him and begin the beat back to the finish line. He never recovered and we won comfortably, much to my relief. Syd was contentedly puffing his pipe on the quayside when we tied up and waved his arm in salute. Bill was happy and so were we.

Our entry fee entitled us to a slap up meal supplied by the pub in the marquee. We woofed down mince and tatties with brown sauce and beer. The drizzle subsided and what must pass for a summer's day in Orkney fanned out, although no one removed their jackets. We stood around on the lawn and Bill stepped up to accept his trophy. Dave and I posed with him for a photo and they were all too polite to mention anything about 'ringers from over the border.'

That night the pub was thronged. Normally, Bill said, you could expect to find no more than seven or eight people there. A woman came up to me. 'Were you on that sailing yacht coming up the Sound today?' I nodded. 'I could see you from my window. You looked magnificent.'

I assumed she was talking about the boat, but just in case she wasn't I beat a discreet retreat. This might have been the once a year day in Longhope, I thought.

We retired to the boat well before the evening reached its raucous conclusion. I'd reckoned we needed to leave at first light to catch the tide for our complicated flight from the clutches of the Orkney currents. That meant us departing at four-thirty. Angus was down at the lifeboat. He wandered over and called down.

'You boys ok? Do you need any more fenders or anything?' I thanked him and said we were fine. I casually mentioned my plans hoping that if I'd made some gross miscalculation he'd correct me.

'Aye, that'll do you,' was all he said, which was good enough for me. We were touched by the warmth of the welcome in this tiny community. It would have been great to have stayed longer.

Twelve

☙

Inshore Forecast for 24 hours from 18.00 6 July 2013
Cape Wrath to Rattray Head including Orkney.
Wind southwest Force 4 or 5, occasionally 6 in north at first.
Sea slight or moderate in east—occasionally very rough west of Orkney.

WE HAD A BROKEN NIGHT. The wind got up and pressed *Shearwater* onto the quay. The tide was ebbing and as we sank down the quayside we had to keep adjusting the height of the tyre fenders. They were full of water and weighed a ton. I fretted as to how we would get the boat off the harbour wall if the wind kept blowing, but it looked kindly on us and faded away just before dawn. I was quite glad when the alarm went and we could set off on the next 'crux move' of the trip—escaping Orkney. The forecast spoke of very rough seas in the western side of Orkney, but the south-westerly winds favoured our passage to Wick on the mainland.

When Steve joined me in Stornoway he'd brought along the Clyde Cruising Club pilot book for Orkney, which was just as well because the pilots I had bought, which purported to cover the north-west, north and north-east Scottish coasts, somewhat infuriatingly ignored the margins between each area, so there was virtually nothing on Cape Wrath and scant else on Orkney itself. However the Clyde pilot was good and gave clear directions for beating the ferocious currents which rip along the Pentland Firth. This stretch of water boasts the strongest tide in Great Britain. The pilot suggested that we should aim to take the last of the ebb westwards to Aith Hope on the southern coast of Hoy and then sail due south. The flood would carry us south east but not so far as to set us on to the islands of Swona and South Ronaldsay. When I ran this past Sean he scoffed and said the sailing directions had been written at a time when yachts had to rely on sail alone and had no engines to get them out of trouble. This was all well and good for a local who knew the eddies, but who was I, with my frail old Bukh and a small propeller, to second-guess the proffered wisdom?

As the sun was poking its head over Flotta we motored down the Sound of Long Hope in a flat calm sea; we turned to starboard to emerge from the islands between Cantick Head and the tiny island of Switha. Despite the calm sea in the approach, between the two points we could see a dark line where the seas were breaking. In the distance we could make out white flashes of waves smashing against the foot of the cliffs on Somay. We hoisted the mainsail and headed out through the gap. There was a huge swell as we motored along the coast to the point where we could bear away to head south. The current swirled the sea in strange patterns, waves rolled in all directions. I couldn't imagine the maelstrom that a gale would create. I studied the chart plotter, anxious to note the point where I could turn *Shearwater* towards the mainland. I put the helm over and almost at once the flood tide seized us. We were heading due south but the instruments showed us to we be making 9.5 knots over the ground towards the south east. In the distance to port the island of Somay sat poised to ensnare us. I notched up the engine revs, keen to make good our escape.

After an hour and half of intense concentration the mainland drew near and we cleared the cliffs of Duncansby Head, and I breathed a sigh of relief. As though it had lost interest in the contest the wind died away and it was almost an anticlimax as we motored down to Wick harbour in flat calm water, mooring on the visitor's pontoon at 11.00. *Shearwater* was back on the mainland. I took a shower and got my head down. The activities of the last couple of days had left me mentally fatigued and I slept like a log. Dave went to try some fishing off the pier. Syd went a-wandering, pipe in hand. I managed a couple of hours of deep sleep and when I woke the sun was doing its best to warm the harbour. I got a text from Keith who was flying up to Wick to join us. He was due to land at four. We walked up to the supermarket to provision up for the week ahead. I could see the airport perimeter fence nearby and suggested Keith got the taxi to pick us up at the supermarket.

It was good to see Keith again. He is one of my oldest pals and a good sailor. After showing him the boat we walked back up into town to Wetherspoons, to catch some of the Wimbledon finals where all the hopes were on the Scottish lad 'our Andy.' We arrived just in time for the final set. I was surprised the pub wasn't more crowded but perhaps tennis wasn't a big thing in the far north of Scotland. Syd arrived and got the next round in. As a keen beer connoisseur he noticed our replacement pints weren't the same as the first round, although the label on the pumps suggested they were. After sticking him out for a bit the bar staff went off to the cellar and came back to acknowledge they'd got the kegs mixed up. We sorted that out and decided to stay for the Sunday roast. Keith ordered and came back to tell us the bad news was that all dinners came with a complimentary pint. We fairly rolled back down to the harbour.

Monday 8 July was a sunny start. The course down the north-east of Scotland comprised a series of hops across Moray Firth and the Firth of Forth. If there had been time we could easily have spent a couple of weeks exploring these areas, but if I was to get to London in a fortnight I had to cut across both of them. We set off for the first long haul across Moray Firth, a distance of sixty five miles. Syd was in full flow most of the time, recounting this and that traveller's tale. I'd heard many of them more than once before and tried in vain to marshal the conversation to include the others who struggled to get a word in. The wind died away after a couple of hours and we motored all day to arrive off Peterhead well after dark. There were heavy ship movements in and out of this busy harbour which nowadays exists primarily to serve the oil rigs. Yachts are just about tolerated and a few pontoons have been established in the far corner. I called up the harbour authority requesting permission to enter.

'Affirmative, *Shearwater*,' came the reply. 'Follow that large vessel now entering the harbour but keep well clear as she will be turning to port.'

I peered over the sprayhood trying to make out the harbour entrance, which was lost amongst the numerous flashing navigation lights. What at first appeared to be a stretch of featureless coastline proved to be the side of an enormous support ship, the very vessel we were commanded to proceed behind. We were much closer to the entrance than I had realised. We followed her in and swung away to starboard to keep out of her way. It took another half hour to make our way around the edge of the harbour and to the corner where we found the marina. We finally moored up at eleven-thirty after a long day.

Dave was occupying the quarter berth, which lies aft behind the navigation table. During the night there was a steady crackle of cellophane as he worked through his store of boiled sweets. We pulled his leg the next morning. We were at last beginning to feel some warmth and I could shed the extra layers that had been obligatory throughout the last few weeks. Dave felt the forestay was a bit saggy when the genoa came under load and suggested we try to tighten it. Keith cooked breakfast while we dismantled the roller furling gear and took a turn on the fore-stay bottle screw. Having witnessed the effects of a forestay failure Dave took a particular interest in this part of the boat. He and Syd, both engineers, rose to the challenge of taking it all apart. When working at the very bow of the boat the biggest danger is to drop some vital part in the water. Fortunately we only managed to do that with a small washer which I replaced from one of the many jars of spares Harry, the previous owner, had left on board.

The plan for the day was a shorter sail down the coast to the tiny harbour of Stonehaven. This would reduce the length of the next long hop across the Firth of Forth. Syd began the day where he had left off. What began as a passing reference to the U-boat drama Das Boot quickly blossomed so that every other comment or nautical term was paraphrased in pidgin German.

'Hey Syd, how about us having a story-free day,' I shouted. 'We've all been around a bit and seen the world.' I immediately regretted it.

'Aye, alright then,' he said and went very silent. The sailing that morning took place in an uncomfortable silence. Syd went and sat on the foredeck and the rest of us made awkward conversation. Dave was very quiet and I felt certain that I'd offended him.

Food is a great healer and over lunch relations thawed, although Syd remained subdued. We entered the tiny harbour at Stonehaven in late afternoon. I called the harbourmaster and on me telling him we were a bilge keeler he directed us to the harbour wall where he normally berthed his own yacht. He'd taken her round to the inner drying harbour to scrub off and antifoul. It suited us fine. The tide was dropping fast making it a long climb up the rusty ladder on the harbour wall.

Syd went off to find a supermarket and to recce the pubs, and we investigated the showers. He returned to pronounce the place suitable for an overnight stay, meaning the beer was up to standard. The pub he favoured overlooked the harbour and as the menu matched the beer we trooped in and ordered. A pretty young lass came over to take our orders and said, 'Evening Gentlemen, and how are you this evening?'

Dave ventured, 'All the better for seeing your smiling face.' She blushed and someone said, 'Watch out, love, if he offers you one of his boiled sweets.' She said nothing and walked off. Dave was mortified and we all cracked up. Spirits were restored.

The next passage across the Firth of Forth was going to be a long one. An absence of wind and adverse tides made for a tedious motor and an uneventful slog. We were glad to arrive at Eyemouth. I'd read about the difficult entrance to this harbour and sure enough it was hard to spot amongst the numerous rocks which bestrew the approach. Ahead of us a largish square-rigged training ship entered the harbour.

'If he had room we should have no problem,' I said.

Once through the entrance we slowly motored down a shallow channel working out where the moorings lay. It's always a puzzle, and part of the pleasure, decoding the directions given in the pilots. I called the harbourmaster who gave me an equally obscure reference, suggesting we look out for a yacht called Sunrise and moor outside her. It was low water and on the tide line, at the foot of some weed covered rocks, a big fat old seal was lounging. He threw us half a glance, quickly realising we wouldn't be providing any fishy titbits. Later, when a fishing boat stole up to the inner fishing quay we saw the seal swimming earnestly in its wake. Talk about a take-out.

Syd announced he was off to get some chips to which, on his return, we added a ready meal, and we had a relaxing supper on board. We'd reached that pleasant stage of the week where the hard passages were behind us and, barring any mishaps or dramatic change in the weather, we were on target to reach our destination for the weekend, North Shields, on the Tyne.

The next morning were up early and off at 07.30 to catch a favourable tide down the coast towards Blyth. We were heading for the pontoons run by the Royal Northumberland Yacht club, which is housed in the last wooden lightship to see service in British waters. It was a straightforward passage and in late afternoon we moored and trogged off to sample what were billed as the finest yachtsmen's showers in the area. They weren't bad, and smelling sweeter we settled down in the club bar for a relaxing pint. The deck rises up to the bow of the lightship, where the saloon bar is situated. The slope is sufficiently great that they have built specially converted bar stools with legs of different lengths. You don't want to get the stool the wrong way round, though. Suitably refreshed we retired to our bunks. Not a bad life.

The next morning we had an easy start. The plan was to sail down the coast, anchoring at the Farne Islands for lunch before heading towards the Quays Marina in North Shields, journey's end for the week. The tide didn't favour us until mid morning so first thing we strolled along the dilapidated wood piling of the quayside and then along the beach to where we found a cafe for breakfast. Groups of young women in jogging suits obediently trotted behind personal trainers. Syd declined the invitation to lead us in a similar exercise.

On the way down from Orkney the Autohelm had been playing up. This device is a godsend when sailing on long passages. It connects to the tiller and holds the given course for as long as you need. Only mine was having a nervous breakdown. After a few minutes' use it began sawing back and forth causing *Shearwater*'s course to resemble the trail of a drunken spider. Before leaving harbour we tried to re-set it and motored slowly round in circles. Anyone watching from the quay would have thought we'd lost it. Needless to say the unit couldn't be pacified and it was consigned to its case, pending further attention from an expert.

One of the books I had on board records the progress of a single hander on passage around the UK. I found his notes on various harbours invaluable but usually couldn't match his passage time. He must have been turbo charged on the trip down the coast to the Farnes, because we anchored at least an hour after his passage time suggested and that was after motoring most of the way. We nosed into the anchorage just off Inner Farne. The trip boats, loaded with passengers out of Seahouses, chugged around the islands, disgorging passengers who scrambled over the rocks, running the gauntlet of angry attention from the tern colony, which clearly resented any visitors from the mainland.

We anchored and cracked open some cans of beer to accompany lunch. I'd always imagined the Farne islands to be magical and was a bit disappointed to find a shallow pile of rocks without any special charm. Keith had sailed past on previous trips, putting in to Holy Isle which from our position looked pretty spectacular, as did the huge castles commanding the coastline. After lunch we didn't tarry long and as soon as the tide gathered pace we weighed anchor and headed for the Tyne. A gentle breeze piped up and we enjoyed one of the few good sails of the week, rounding up at the entrance between the tall towers, under the watchful gaze of the castle at Tynemouth. Something was happening there, the towers of the castle being festooned with enormous medieval banners which shook vigorously in the breeze.

We stowed the sails and entered the historic river, first seeking permission from Tyne VTS which controls all the marine traffic. I contacted the marina where we planned to berth for the weekend and they directed us to the waiting berth in front of the lock. In a trice we were up through the gates and moored to a well maintained pontoon. Job done for the week. The marina put me in touch with a local firm of marine electricians who sent an engineer down that afternoon to look at the Autohelm. Needless to say, it wouldn't repeat its antics and he declared it fit for service—and refused payment.

In the evening we took the taxi into Tynemouth, enjoying the driver's tips as to which parts of the Tyne were 'magic' and which were 'rubbish,' all delivered in singsong Geordie. I texted a pal who hails from Sunderland and told him we were in North Shields. He replied with dire warnings if we strayed into town at night. It felt like we were entering an urban jungle, where each tribe jealously protected its territory and feared the neighbours.

We survived the trip into Tynemouth, and joined the crowds who were out for Friday night in the pubs. They were all dressed to kill and knocking back the beer as though it was going out of fashion. We walked towards the castle and the swirling banners, to discover that Tynemouth was celebrating a music festival. That night a semi-famous seventies band was headlining. One of the policemen patrolling outside the castle pointed out to us a pub overlooking the stage where we could hear the concert for free. We quaffed a pint and stared down from the cliffs into the sandy bay where youngsters revelled on the beach, including one couple who were frolicking in the North Sea fully clothed. We couldn't imagine what they were on.

On Saturday morning I performed my usual role cooking breakfast while the chaps packed. Keith and Syd shared a taxi to the train station. It was a warm sunny day, so much so that whilst I was in Tesco getting the provisions I acquired a new pair of shorts and some flip flops. I've always been a big spender when it comes to clothes. When I got back to the boat Dave had washed the decks and spruced up *Shearwater*. He was staying until Sunday to meet up with the next week's crew and drive their car back to Derbyshire. For the leg down to London the crew was a bit special, because it included Harry, *Shearwater*'s former owner. I was anxious that he would approve of the alterations I'd made and spent most of the day cleaning and polishing whilst listening to the test match on the radio. I managed a snooze in the sunny cockpit, whilst Dave wandered off to explore the hinterland. I said if he hadn't returned in a couple of hours I'd send out a search party.

Walking from the boat to the marina office was, unexpectedly one of the more hazardous parts of the whole trip. Between the pontoons and the lock gates a riot of terns had created a nest site. No doubt there is a proper collective noun but 'riot' seemed to best describe their behaviour. They guarded this area so aggressively that on either end of the pontoon the marina staff had deposited hard hats and umbrellas to protect heads of passers-by from attack by the wheeling and squawking birds.

The marina staff couldn't have been friendlier. They were delighted when I told them *Shearwater* was normally berthed in one of their sister marinas. By now I was beginning to get a reaction when I explained where we'd sailed from. Everyone seems to have wanted to do the trip I was making. I asked where we should go to eat on a Saturday night.

'You've got to visit Gateshead. It's stonking on a Saturday, pet,' said the woman in the marina office.

'Is there a train?' I asked.

'Aye, but you'd be better taking a taxi. It's a bit rough around the station.'

Dave and I couldn't find an armed guard at short notice so we booked a taxi. In broad dialect the driver talked animatedly about the test cricket he'd been watching all day. He wished us a pleasant evening and left us with the usual warning.

'Make sure you get a taxi back to the marina. It gets a bit wild on a Saturday, thou knows?'

We posed for photos in front of the Millennium Bridge, below the magnificent

Sage concert building. I say magnificent but apparently it's adored and despised in equal measure by the good folk of Tyneside. We thought Norman Foster had made a pretty good job of it but such is the lot of a modern architect, I suppose. We walked across the bridge and found a bistro overlooking the river. We chatted through the week that had passed. I was relieved that Dave had enjoyed the trip, particularly our racing exploits in the Longhope regatta. He told me his father had been a shipwright in Newcastle and often talked about a beer called *Cameron's Strong Arm*. Dave was keen to sample some if we could find it. This provided no better excuse than we needed to join the party-goers in Newcastle. After climbing the steep steps to view the castle (the new one from which the city takes its name) we were directed to the Parador, a classic old city bar with a long counter, colourful leaded lights and dark wood panelling. Best of all it was a real ale Mecca. Syd would have been in seventh heaven, we said, as we scratched our chins wondering which to sample first. An enquiry for Cameron's revealed it was no longer being brewed, which was a shame.

When we returned to the streets a full-scale party was underway. Hens joshed with stags. Dave was propositioned by a bride-to-be sporting an enormous pink inflatable phallus. Despite his meek protests I captured the moment on my phone camera. We turned down some free tickets to a gentlemen's club and headed to the Spanish Bar on the waterfront for a coffee and cognac, served in pre-warmed brandy snifters. We caught a taxi back through the jungle and landed safely in the marina, feeling as though we'd had a good night out.

Thirteen

ᛣᚱ

On Sunday Dave packed his kit once again. He wasn't due to join the boat again until Scilly, for the last leg back up to Bristol; we both had unfinished business on the north Cornish coast. Harry and Barry phoned to say they expected to arrive at lunch time. I suggested we could meet them on the fuel pontoon on the river side of the lock. The weather was fair for a short sail down the coast to Hartlepool which would give us a flying start to the next week's passage down the East coast and up the Thames to London. The weather had been very kind so far on the passage from Scotland and I didn't want to waste any of it.

I booked a lock out and thanked the marina for a short but pleasant stay enjoying traditional Geordie hospitality. The marina wished me well and as we slid out of the lock I heard a shout and looked up to see Harry beaming down. We tied up at the fuel berth, and twiddled our thumbs whilst a dive boat took on fourteen hundred pounds worth of fuel. We managed forty. While this was taking place the crews performed the slickest changeover of the trip. Dave waved us off and we headed out into the Tyne. Whilst I helmed us down to the river the lads stowed their gear and once through the entrance we hoisted sail to reach the down the coast to Hartlepool. Another week was under way.

Harry was keen to know all the adventures to date. He looked around the cockpit, nodding in approval at the various improvements. It was a peaceful Sunday afternoon sail and almost too soon we were rounding up outside the entrance to Hartlepool. The harbour walls were crowded with anglers as we made our approach. They seemed reluctant to reel in their lines and when we entered the lock I noticed the anchor was ensnared with a long length of nylon. Someone must have been cursing but it was hardly our fault.

The marina had a reputation as being a splendid affair. It might have been when first opened but a few years on it was looking very tired. Shops lining the side of the marina were boarded up, those remaining open were scruffy. An air of despondency hung over the place.

When the tide turned we motored out of the harbour past the splendid Trincomalee, Britain's oldest floating wooden warship. She dates back to the Napoleonic era and now occupies pride of place in the historic quay centre. We waved at the anglers on the end of the pier and set a course for Whitby. It wasn't a long passage and for once I could take my time. The sun climbed in the sky and we enjoyed a gentle sail along the coast, making the most of the breeze which blew fitfully. We meandered past a wind farm, watching the enormous generator blades limber up for their day's labour.

The North Sea is full of oil and gas platforms and, more recently, wind farms. It remained to be seen whether these vast constructions would be an aid to navigation or tiresome obstructions. The wind freshened and headed us, making for a good beat, although the tide direction was foul all the way. In late afternoon I noticed smoke on the coastline at odds with our wind direction and shortly after the wind veered dramatically and for the last two hours we enjoyed a fast broad reach, probably the first for me in over thirteen hundred miles. It backed again about three miles from Whitby so we motored the last stretch. Soon enough the long tall arms of the harbour entrance at Whitby loomed out of the haze. I thought of another Ogston sailing friend, David, who'd particularly wanted to join us on this leg as he fancied sailing into Whitby dressed in full Dracula costume. Family commitments had forced him to cancel, denying us this spectacle.

We joined other yachts moored at the fisherman's quay all waiting for the tide to rise sufficiently to gain access to the inner harbour. We tied up alongside a large Dutch catamaran which had sailed up the coast that day from the Humber. The skipper said the wind had been so fickle he'd only managed to average five knots, no more than us, which was surprising. Other Dutch craft arrived and, I realised this was their equivalent of the French cruising grounds we used to explore when we berthed in Dartmouth. In the harbour, rowing gigs, crewed by keen youngsters and burly pub teams, practised their racing. We urged on a boat full of buxom lasses being exalted to expend their last ounce of energy by a fearsome looking tattooed woman cox. Excited youths dared each other to plunge into the harbour from the edge of the quay. We sat contentedly, chatting to the Dutch crew, whose perfect English was humbling.

The radio crackled to life and suddenly there was movement on the lifting bridge and all hell broke loose. We were on the outside but already the inner craft had cast off. We slipped our lines and motored off only to be overhauled by several Dutch craft racing each other through the bridge. We let them go and exchanged bemused observations with the harbour staff leaning over the edge of the bridge.

'Just moor where you find a space, lads,' one of them shouted. 'Don't know what all the fuss is about.'

We found a spare pontoon and moored. The shower block was nearby, and suitably refreshed we headed off to the old town. Barry knew it well and took us to his favourite pub overlooking the harbour, where we dined regally and enjoyed some good people-watching. An animated blonde beauty was seeking to impress her man and a Dutch couple who had been walking coast to coast chatted to us, again of course in our native tongue.

We discussed the plans for the next day's passage, which would be one of the longest legs of the trip, cutting across the Wash and round Norfolk to Lowestoft. There were harbours in between but all of them offered patchy shelter, and either dried out or involved detours up rivers which would make the overall journey much longer. Our aim was to get up the Thames to London by the weekend. During the night our pontoon was busy with fishing boats preparing for their night's work, but I'd grown used to these nocturnal noises and slept soundly.

We were up early next morning, provisioning for an overnight passage and topping up the fresh water tank. We'd not used much fuel in the last two days and I still had a spare can of diesel in the locker. The marina office hadn't opened by the time the siren flashed to signal the raising of the bridge. I radioed the harbour control on the way out.

'I haven't been able to pay my harbour dues, yet. The office hasn't opened.' They were relaxed and asked me to phone back later. We cleared the harbour and raised the mainsail. The wind was scant and on the nose so we dropped the sails and motored, keen to make the most of the flood tide. The grand hotels of Scarborough slipped by. We settled into a relaxed routine; Harry of course knew the

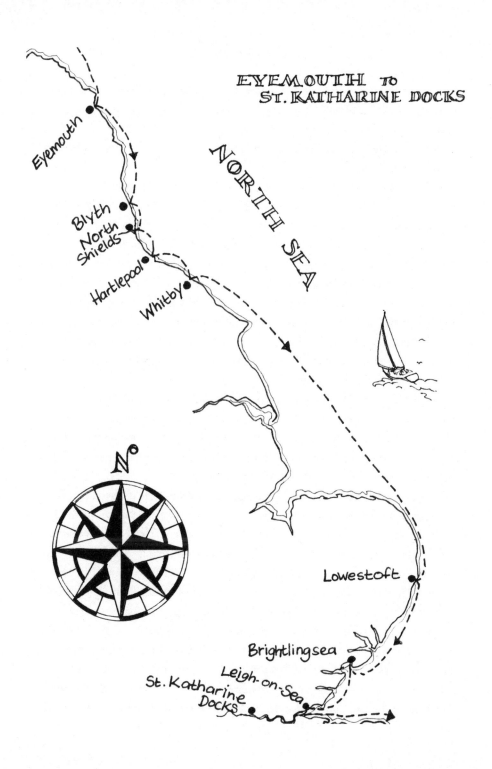

EYEMOUTH to
ST. KATHARINE DOCKS

NORTH SEA

Eyemouth

Blyth
North
Shields

Hartlepool
Whitby

N°

Lowestoft

Brightlingsea
Leigh-on-Sea
St. Katharine
Docks

boat better than I did and Barry, although not experienced in big boats, is a good dinghy sailor. I'd learned to spot early on who moved confidently around the boat and felt very comfortable with my crew.

Barry amused us by referring regularly to the maps in the back of an old diary he'd brought along.

'Which road do you suggest I take after Scarborough?' I quipped.

Our course followed the line of the coast until we reached Bridlington. Then we swung southeast and set a course for the long haul across the Wash. We had to keep a sharp lookout for ships entering and leaving the Humber. The wind was fickle and we motored throughout most of the day. The seas were calm and the sun shone. Harry's wife had sent along a chicken stew which was very welcome, and in the evening we treated ourselves to a glass of wine to accompany the sunset. The evening forecast contained no ominous warnings and we settled into a watch routine similar to that I'd employed with Chris and Dave on our passage up the Irish Sea, all those weeks before. The nights were shorter now and the fair weather maximised the daylight.

Over the years I've always experienced a chill at the moment the sun sets, which I believe is down to the dew point. Once the sun has disappeared it invariably warms up again. Nevertheless sailing at night always demands the right attire. Damp seems to penetrate your very core. I wore long thermal pants and two fleeces under my heavy weather jacket and trousers.

We dodged amongst the gas platforms, each one emitting its own identifying light signal. On the horizon I spotted a ship heading towards us and using the AIS called up the bridge on the VHF. The deck officer said he would alter course 10°. At one point we encountered a large fishing fleet but sailing so far off shore we were spared the curse of the lobster pot buoys.

Early in the early morning off Cromer it became clear that our course would take us through a wind farm. I double checked the sailing directions to make sure we were permitted to sail amongst the pylons. The minimum height under the sweeping arms is about twenty metres (and the height of *Shearwater*'s mast and hull, known as her air draft, is fifteen metres). Despite that knowledge, a bit like when you are sailing under a bridge, there never feels to be enough clearance. Fortunately the tide and wind were slack and we could sail down a channel between the towers, without any threat of being swept onto one. It was very eerie sailing amongst these giants.

Once clear of the wind farm we set a course for Winterton, about the closest you get to a headland along this blunt edge of the land. As we closed the Norfolk coast it was sad to see the houses fighting for survival against a receding coastline. Some of them were now perched on the very edge of the cliffs and I suspected did not have long before a strong gale would wash away their foundations. The morning wore on and the sun shone dutifully, but the tide resisted our desire to sail past the east cardinal mark off Winterton, quaintly called 'Cockle.' Rounding it would have been more than enough to warm the cockles of my heart. Slowly the wind filled in from the east but it was well after lunch before we could ease the sheets and close-reach down the coast past Yarmouth and on to Lowestoft. There were numerous sandbanks around the entrance and I had to be careful not to let fatigue lull us into a navigational error and run aground just short of our destination.

As we approached the harbour I could make out the Sparrownest, a building which houses the Royal Naval Patrol Museum, recording the history of the minesweepers based in Lowestoft. My father served there during the War. It was only the year previously, and after his death, that I discovered the existence of the place and brought my mother up for a couple of days. Armed with crumpled old cuttings and photos she passed a touching couple of hours chatting to the aged volunteers who ran the place. I radioed the port authority for permission to enter the harbour and was instructed to follow an old gaffer sedately making her approach. A French yacht cut in front of us at a great rate of knots. Just like a supermarket car park in Nice, I thought.

Inside the harbour we headed for the old dock and the visitors' pontoons run by the Royal Norfolk and Suffolk Yacht Club. With its long bowsprit and deep keel the old gaffer was struggling to manoeuvre in the tight confines of the harbour. We stood off and then reversed out of the entrance to give her more room. Meanwhile the French yacht was remonstrating with the berthing master and shot off from his allocated berth in search of something better, gesturing wildly to us that we should take his place. It looked like a new boat but he seemed to be making a meal of it. His space suited us and we moored up and shook hands. Another key passage under our belts. We were tired but content.

The clubhouse was a splendid Edwardian building, oozing character and testament to an age when yachting was the preserve of the wealthy. The menu looked appetizing so, after a long shower, we relaxed on the sun deck with a pint of best Norfolk bitter. I went to pay my berthing dues and noticed the berthing master's daybook. Alongside the entry for the French yacht he'd written 'arrogant bastard.' I suppose it was one way to vent his frustration. The food matched the promise of the menu and we retired happily to our bunks and slept well.

The next morning we had a lazy start. The tide would not turn in our favour until mid-morning so Barry wandered into town to buy provisions and Harry supervised me fitting a part to the engine. The sea fret which plagues the east coast in the summer had burned off by the time we'd refuelled and cast off. I set a course down the coast towards Brightlingsea, which was in easy range of the Thames where I wanted to be on Friday for my important rendezvous. The wind was fresh and obligingly backed to the north-east giving us a delightful broad reach. For the first time since Oban I was able to set the spinnaker. The sun beamed down and we savoured a creamy sail in the company of the old gaffer and another classic yacht. When you find yourself on the same course as another yacht it's impossible to resist the temptation to match your speed if not race the other. The big quadrilateral mainsails of old classic yachts are ideal for downwind sailing, and it was only our lighter displacement which kept us in touch.

The famous rivers and harbours of Suffolk came and went. I remembered fondly my exploits on this stretch of coast as a young man, and wished yet again that I had the time to linger. The river Deben, and Waldringfield on it, were jewels where I could have spent a few days. Brightlingsea lies on the river Colne which itself merges with the Blackwater a few miles from where it exits into the North Sea amid a jumble of sand banks. Despite a favourable tide and good boat speed I realised it would be dark before we made our way up the river. Closing the Blackwater it was difficult to make out the marks against the low sun in the sky. Reluctantly we dropped the spinnaker, as the breeze had gradually increased and would be much stronger when we altered course to make landfall.

I made detailed notes of the light characteristics of all the navigation buoys we would need to identify to safely negotiate the tricky entrance. The chart showed the tangle of mud banks which would snare us given the chance. The sun was setting when, in the last of the daylight, I took up the binoculars to confirm the position of the Knoll, a north cardinal buoy and the leading mark for our entrance. Under mainsail alone with the engine ticking over to give us extra power if need be we raced across the shallows and rounded the buoy, which was heeling over in the strong current.

At the entrance to the Colne the dark shapes of the emerging sand banks on either side confirmed the tide was dropping fast. I realised that if we ran aground now we would not be able to refloat until the next tide which would seriously compromise our plans for the following day. Harry took the helm, his eyes glued to the dull red glow of the steering compass. I sang out the course alterations and distances to the next mark and Barry sat at the chart table watching our progress on the chart plotter, shouting the equivalent of 'left a bit' when he thought appropriate. The channel grew more and more narrow, the water more shallow. I was confident we would have enough tide to reach the deep pool of the pontoons off the town but it was nerve-racking stuff. We strained our eyes to filter out the navigation buoy lights from glow of the street lamps in the town. The final approach beacons blinked to beckon us on and suddenly we had arrived. It was not immediately clear where the pontoons were. On all side mud banks rose up. I scrutinised the chart, anxiously struggling to match the contours to what we could make out under the beam of the spotlight Harry played on the shore.

'I've got it,' I said. 'Steer for that solid white light. It marks the outer end of the pontoons.'

We crept forward, not wishing to mess up at the final point. Dark shapes ahead materialised into fishing craft and a bright light at one end proved to emanate from a trawler unloading its catch. I saw a space behind her and edged *Shearwater* alongside.

'Are we ok here for the night?' I enquired.

'You'll do right enough there old son,' came the reply.

We made fast and slipped below for a coffee and a nightcap of best malt.

'That was interesting,' said Harry. I smiled.

'Nice one lads. Great sail. No rush in the morning. It's only thirty miles to Southend and the tide doesn't turn until midday. Another lazy start.'

I awoke at the start of what I had always imagined to be an exciting day. I was born in Leigh-on-Sea, and from the outset I planned to call in at Bell Wharf in old Leigh. The idea was to head for Ray Gut, a creek separating a sandbank on the edge of the Thames from the mud flats of Southend on Sea. We would take the evening tide into Leigh and collect my sister, Marian, who had always wanted to travel by boat up the Thames to Tower Bridge and St Katherine's dock, our final destination for the week. In my youth the bay at Southend had seemed like the ocean itself but in reality it is a very shallow area which dries extensively, the mud flats extending almost to the end of the pier, itself over a mile long.

In order to arrive at the right time we needed to take the whole of the flood tide down past the river Crouch and around the corner at Foulness. We would then skirt the Maplin Sands and the other sand banks which festoon the entrance to the Thames, and which have become the graveyard of many ships throughout history.

We could shave a few miles off the passage by taking the Wallet Spitway at the mouth of the Blackwater, cutting between two sandbanks and avoiding a course north east and round the outside. I quizzed a fisherman as to whether I could get safely cross the bar at low water.

'What d'yer draw, son?' he asked.

'Just over a meter,' I replied in the tone of pupil to schoolmaster. He nodded solemnly. There was an hour to kill so after breakfast we took the water taxi across to the little town and wandered the harbour admiring the superb classic east coast craft nestling in their mud berths. Tanned sails, wooden spars and beautiful lines epitomise the scenery of east coast harbours. The yacht club was another Edwardian splendour with ivy trickling from crafted walls. The Main Street was lined with cottages constructed of traditional overlapping timber and terracotta pantile roofs. We easily could have squandered the rest of the day, but London beckoned.

I paid our dues in the little harbour office and we took the water taxi back to *Shearwater*, lying patiently in her berth. There was more tide than when we had crept up the creek the night before, and a lot more daylight. We let go to join the small crowd of yachts savouring the fresh breeze. I relished the chance of another good day's sailing and to rest the engine. My only hesitation was the sea state over the bar at the Wallet Spitway. We re-traced our passage of the night before until I judged it right to bear away to the south. Ahead of us the sand banks were exposed and the Wallet fizzed beneath a short sea. *Shearwater* ploughed into the chop and I held my breath as the numbers on the echo sounder steadily dropped. 4 metres, 3.5, 3. *Shearwater* could hit the bottom if any of the troughs fell too deep. We held our nerve and grinned in relief when at last the depth increased and the sea grew less agitated. I set a course for the mouth of the Thames. We were on our way.

The breeze and favourable tide were powerful enough to speed us along under genoa alone. The sandbanks on either side bristled with noisy seagulls and seals basking at the edge of the tide. The low marshes of Essex lay on our starboard side, a wind farm was exercising vigorously and over on the Kent coast the cliffs of North Foreland trembled in the heat haze. The high-rise flats of Southend appeared on the horizon and I began to make out familiar landmarks: the remains of a wartime defence boom which once stretched across the mouth of the Thames, now only an ugly string of concrete pillars jutting out into the sea; we could make out Southend pier and a posse of kite surfers blasted up and down, one of them carving a wake around our stern.

As we creamed past the pier head I partially furled the genoa to slow us down. What as a youth had seemed to be a wide anchorage now appeared on the chart as not much more than a graze in the thick glutinous mud. We picked out the Ray Gut buoy and sidled forward, almost feeling our way to the deepest point in the anchorage. I went forward and prepared the hook and we let go the chain in 5 metres. Harry put the engine astern and almost immediately the anchor bit and the chain rose up taut. Nothing could be as assured as the ground holding in the thick mud of the Thames. I recounted to the chaps tales of my boyhood, at low tide walking out across the mud flats to bail the dinghy and sliding my boots across the surface to avoid sinking in.

The plan was to have a bite of supper and wait for the rising tide to cover the mudflats and then steal into Leigh. I realised it would probably be dark by then but hoped the lights of the shore would prove sufficient. We would then retreat to the Ray and anchor again to await the last of the ebb tide and then carry the full flood for forty miles up to Tower Bridge. It was a first visit for the crew. I pointed out the remains of the Norman castle at Hadleigh and the old town of Leigh where cockle boats unload their hard-won sweepings. High water was due at 22.00 but we were on neaps, the lowest high water in the month. There seemed a general lack of the stuff. At 20.30 I phoned my brother, Paul, who still lives locally.

'Hi mate, I'm thinking of heading in now. I'm not sure we're going to get much more tide and if I go aground I want a chance of refloating,' I said.

'Ok, just follow the buoys that mark Leigh creek. They're all port hand and unlit. When you get to the last bend, close in to the foreshore, turn sharply to port and head up to Bell Wharf. We'll be waiting.'

I entered a waypoint on the chart plotter so I could return to the same point to re-anchor. If there was enough water now I could use the same position later. We raised the anchor and motored slowly across to pick up the first of the red can buoys marking the creek, and almost immediately the depth of water plummeted to three metres. We were still about three quarters of a mile off shore which was not very encouraging.

We assumed the same roles as the night before, only this time there were no lights to help us identify the buoys. Harry said it was 'mark one eyeball stuff.' This time we had much less water to begin with and Barry was kept very busy shouting up suggested course alterations. It was a bit much to expect the plotter to report our position to such accuracy, so we relied more on the depth sounder, swerving to port or starboard to seek out the deepest water in the creek. Slowly we edged towards the penultimate bend. I could see Bell Wharf and high above the tower of Leigh Church, yards from my birthplace. *Shearwater* draws 1.2 metres so when the depth sounder shows that or less we are about to touch.

It was growing dark more quickly than I'd hoped, which made identifying the unlit buoys even more difficult. I looked down towards the shore. On our port side we crept past two can buoys. Just one more bend.

'Which buoy should I steer for, Rod?' asked Harry. I peered ahead and saw a clutch of four buoys.

'Search me, I can't see which is the turning buoy,' I murmured.

'1 metre; now it's 0.9.'

We lurched to a halt.

'We're aground,' shouted Harry.

I cursed. All that way and we run aground metres from my home town quay. Thank heavens it's dark, I thought.

'What are we doing, skipper?' asked Harry, shaking me out of my stupor.

'Assuming we can get off, we'll have to abandon it. There's just not enough tide.'

Harry waggled the rudder back and forth whilst giving the engine some exercise in reverse. I phoned my brother, 'It isn't going to happen, Bruv. There's not enough water. I don't want to spend the night stuck on the mud. I'll miss the tide up to London.'

'Don't fret,' he said. 'I'll see if the yacht club can run Marian out to you.'

He rang off and whilst we extricated ourselves from the mud bank my good old brother trotted along the tow path with Marian. My brother-in-law Bob, and Mum on her pavement scooter, tagged along behind. They must have covered the 400 metres or so in record time because no sooner had we re-floated the boat and gingerly edged back into deeper water than I spotted the bow wave of a yacht tender bashing through the waves, carrying my brother and sister. In a jiffy they drew alongside and we hauled Marian on to the side deck.

'Welcome aboard,' I said, hugging her.

I made some hasty introductions and we beat a retreat back out to the Ray Gut, where I was grateful to find a spoonful more water into which we dropped the anchor. Not for the first time in the day I pondered what a piddly puddle I'd spent my early days sailing in. We settled our nerves with coffee and a malt.

'If we get up at very first light, assuming we can find our way out of here, we can stem the last of the ebb for an hour,' I said. 'Then we can take all the flood up to London.'

'So what time will that be, skipper?' asked Harry.

'I'll set the alarm for 04.00,' I replied.

'Better get to bed,' said Barry.

Marian took the fore-cabin and I wriggled into the quarter-berth. I felt disappointed that we'd not got alongside Bell Wharf, but relieved that the passage to London was still on. At one point I heard waves slapping on the hull and feared we were aground. I jumped on deck to find the wind was holding the boat across the tide. I hardly shut my eyes again before the alarm jolted me awake. I roused

the others and put on the kettle. It wasn't exactly first light but the cloud was beginning to reflect the sunrise. We raised the anchor and motored slowly towards
the pier head. There still seemed to be precious little water and Barry was kept
busy once more shouting up the course corrections. On a few occasions the depth
sounder edged perilously close to 1 meter but gratefully we reached the entrance
buoy and found deeper water on the edge of the dredged channel of the Thames.

By the time the sun graced us with an appearance all was well with the world.
We were motoring in deep water with a flood tide sweeping us towards our destination. We passed under the Queen Elizabeth Bridge with the M25 traffic thun-
dering overhead. We munched on bacon sandwiches and in no time at all I was
calling up the control officer to request permission to transit the Thames Barrier.

'*Shearwater*, affirmative. Take gate Alpha. Keep to the starboard side of the
river at all times and keep a sharp lookout.'

We dutifully obeyed and rounded the next bend to see ahead of us the massive tower of Canary Wharf. It was only nine o'clock and the first lock into St
Kat's was not until ten thirty. There was a risk of us arriving too early so we
throttled back and used what little wind there was to coast up under foresail.
Most of the lower Thames is pretty industrial, and names like Coalhouse Point,
Gravesend and Mucking are the legacy of a time when the river was the sewer,
drain and burial place for the inhabitants of the capital. But the upper reaches are
splendid, with magnificent views of buildings such as the Royal Observatory and
the former naval college at Greenwich with its stately white stone columns. This
was where Nelson's body was brought ashore prior to his funeral. We marvelled
at the best of the modern riparian architecture and scorned the worst of the concrete abominations.

All too soon the climax of the week's trip arrived. Ahead of us Tower Bridge
stood majestically blocking our passage. Famous ships and those favoured with
special arrangements can book for the bridge to be raised, gaining access to the
Pool of London. For us it was enough to have arrived, just two weeks to the day
since *Shearwater* had departed Stromness in Orkney. I puffed with pride. We
called up the marina staff and were asked to stand by, which involved motoring
slowly up and down outside the lock entrance, stemming the fast flowing tide and
dodging the high speed ferries, trip boats and commercial barges, not to mention

the fleet of yachts from a small motor boat club which had also booked into the harbour for the weekend.

We watched as umpteen craft were summoned to enter the lock, not believing there'd be room for us. But we did get a call and tucked in between two yachts which had made the passage up from the Blackwater. The huge lock gate swung shut and water flooded to raise us up to dock level. We all got a berth, which for us necessitated tucking into a space which the skipper of the adjoining yacht thought improbable. As the boat glided into its berth Harry and I exchanged a smile of satisfaction. *Shearwater* had arrived in London, still on schedule.

In truth I was exhausted. The constant process of passage planning, tidal calculations and weather forecasting had caught me up, and the closer I got to achieving my ambitions the more jealously I was guarding against failure. Still, we were in London, moored opposite one of the most picturesque pubs, in one of the most famous docks, under the gaze of one of the most famous iconic monuments in the world.

Paul met us for lunch before taking Marian back to Leigh. Like the rest of the crew she was weary from the early start and the excitement of it all, but pleased she'd taken part. It had been the perfect week, starting off with our flyer down to Hartlepool on Sunday, the good winds, great harbours, the excitement of sailing amongst the wind farms, even the attempt to get into Leigh. It was everything I had hoped for and the company had been great. I was relieved and pleased in equal measure that Harry appreciated my further restoration of *Shearwater*. I badly needed some sleep and after lunch took a couple of hours' siesta. I awoke feeling not much better but strong tea and fruit cake restored some energy. That evening Harry, Barry and I strolled across Tower Bridge to dine in a pleasant Italian restaurant overlooking the river. On the way back we stared down from the floodlit structure to marvel at the majestic beauty of London to which my faithful old boat had borne us.

Fourteen

❧

Andy and his son Tom, part of the crew for the following week, called to say they were in London. I asked them if they could arrive the following day when the fourth member, David, would be joining us. I desperately needed an hour or two to myself. I had to change the engine oil. In our dash south I'd run the engine for 100 hours. The least I could do for the old lady was to keep her serviced regularly, in a manner of speaking. The task I'd approached with caution a few weeks before I now carried out almost without thinking. I was even able to plug the phone into the boat Hi-Fi and chat to Jan as I changed the oil filter.

The following week we had a long passage ahead of us, to Dartmouth. David Gill is an old friend who still keeps a boat at Kingswear, where Jan and I began our offshore sailing. He was happy to choose this leg as he could arrange for his wife (also Jan) to meet us. They live not far from us and it was suggested that my Jan would drive his wife down to join us for the weekend. It would have been helpful to have locked out on the Sunday and start down the Thames that day, but I couldn't bring myself to leave so quickly. The sun was red hot and I rigged up the cockpit tent as a sun shade. I'd never thought it would serve as such when we were trying to stem the leaks from the rain in Cardiff.

The crew mix for the week was potentially the most difficult of the trip. Andy from Ogston, who I hardly knew, was bringing along Tom, his teenage son. Andy had bought his own boat the year before but I sensed didn't have much experience and Tom was along for the education. At the other extreme David, who was highly experienced, was the wrong side of seventy and volunteered that his wife didn't feel confident to sail with him any longer. I just hoped I could blend this team.

David snored soundly and got up four times in the night for a pee. I thought I was bad. Tom was a nice lad and Andy was hard to fathom. Nevertheless this was the crew for the week and we had a long trip ahead of us. We arranged with the marina to take the first lock out on the Monday, leaving mid morning. We crammed in with a Thames barge and some of the small boat club and a 40 footer who knocked me sideways when the skipper asked, 'Does this boat hail from Poole?'

'It does. I bought her last year,' I replied.

'I thought I recognised her. Were the decks and sail covers once green by any chance?'

It turned out he knew well the previous owner to Harry. I didn't let on that Harry had told me she was in a state when he acquired her but perhaps the guy knew that anyway because as we parted he said, 'You've done a fantastic job on her.' Nice.

My plan was to get a flyer by bucking the last of the flood tide but it backfired and we made painfully slow progress, about an hour later being overhauled by more powerful yachts that had locked out after us. On top of that an easterly wind blew strongly making it difficult to tack in the confined waters. I recalled years ago on my previous exit from the Thames in another boat when again I'd been forced to battle an easterly wind, although then it had been April and bitterly cold. This time it was so warm we sailed with the sprayhood down.

I noticed David was somewhat slow about the boat. He relied on the grab rails to heave himself upright. I recognised the signs by now. He also made continual use of the pilot book but when asked could never find me any useful information. Tom was very keen, darting about the boat clutching his iPad which he used to predict to the minute when we would be arriving where, and Andy was instructing Tom. I felt as though we were sailing the boat by committee and just hoped it would settle down.

In early evening we picked up a mooring buoy off Queenborough, on the Swale, near the mouth of the Medway. I went forward with Tom to pick up the buoy leaving Andy on the helm. He misjudged the way *Shearwater* carries and overshot by a mile. I took the helm and we circled round, much to the amusement of the crew of a French yacht on the next mooring. Then, to my irritation I discovered that Andy had somehow contorted my shopping list to leave us short of ready meals. We got round it with potatoes and tinned vegetables but it added to the frustration. It felt as though it was going to be a long week.

We enjoyed a peaceful night on the mooring. The sound of the oyster catchers and other marsh birds was a poignant reminder of the sailing days of my youth. The next morning the crew went ashore to get more provisions (with more explicit instructions). They came back saying the town was dire, comprising a boarded-up pub and closed shops. They even had to buy tokens to get back through a turnstile at the head of the mooring pontoon. Perhaps it was to discourage townsfolk from fleeing.

We set off for Ramsgate. The wind was light but useable. We skirted past the wreck of the *Richard Montgomery*, a munitions ship that foundered on a sand bank during the war, and which nobody dare touch because the explosives are thought to be 'unstable.' This is a euphemism for saying that if it went up it would smash most of the windows in Southend, five miles away across the Thames. I introduced the crew to my concertina. I thought I was making progress but the response was pretty flat. I plotted a course to maximally utilize the ebb in the main channel of the Thames, if there is such a thing. It's a testament to the skill of the river pilots that such enormous ships regularly navigate up the shallow waters of the Thames. It was important to arrive off North Foreland before the tide turned. We altered course to the south at slack water. It meant we were entering Ramsgate at low water so once again we had to skirt the sand banks in the approaches. A pilot vessel, with local knowledge, roared along the coast inshore but he was going too fast for us to follow so we took the longer route round.

I called up the fuel berth operators using the number obtained from the latest edition of the South Coast Pilot.

'Is that Ramsgate fuel berth?' I asked. There was a pause,

'It was, but about thirteen years ago.'

So much for buying the latest edition of the book, I thought. When we arrived in the harbour I was told the marina fuel berth would open at 07.30 the next morning. This was later than I wanted because we would lose most of the flood sweeping down the Channel, but we needed diesel. I'd ducked the opportunity to re-fuel on the Thames because the fuel berth just below Tower Bridge is prone to violent wash from the excursion boats roaring up and down. We would have got smashed to pieces if we'd been alongside at the wrong moment.

We showered, found the yacht club and enjoyed a pint before trying out the recommended Thai restaurant. I suggested we should be away and moored to the fuel berth first thing the next morning so we would be certain to be the first boat served. The crew responded and were all up and about bright and early. I suggested they should top up the water tanks. This was done with much shouting and I realised they were likely to disturb the adjoining boats. I bit my tongue at first, only to have a minor paddy when David couldn't work out how to uncoil the hose. This was becoming a self fulfilling prophecy. Andy quite rightly rebuked me for my impatience.

We motored round to the fuel berth and tied up. By 07.50 no one had shown up and when the guy did finally amble down the ladder he couldn't find the keys to unlock the pumps. We finally left a couple of hours later than I wanted. The plan was to head towards Brighton or Eastbourne. I favoured the former, because I knew the entrance. David had moored before at Eastbourne and we decided to see what progress we made before making a final choice. Just to be perverse the wind had veered round to the south-west, on the nose for the passage along the coast. We motor-sailed down to Dover, a lumpy sea causing *Shearwater*'s engine to stall, and we fetched up close to the entrance to the harbour, where I had to request permission from the traffic control to make sure we weren't crawling across when one of the cross-channel ferries shot out. This operation took about half an hour and by then the ebb had lost any benefit. We slogged down the coast to Folkestone by which time a strong wind had whipped up the sea. I tried to set a course to beat into the bay, hoping to dodge some of the tide, but David pointed out we had to head much more into the teeth of the wind if we were to round Dungeness. There was nothing for it but to hand the mainsail and motor head on into the wind and waves.

At the head of Dungeness Point stands the power station, its massive chimney sneering at all passers-by, or so it seemed. We had plenty of time to take it all in, making pitiful progress until the tide turned in early evening. We were then able to hoist the sails again, bear away slightly and take the tide. A warm meal restored spirits and we discussed our options. If we were to make Dartmouth by the weekend we couldn't afford to lose time in harbour and I suggested we sailed through the night and put in at Poole on the Thursday. This would then give us a fighting chance of making Dartmouth by the weekend. Andy and Tom liked the prospect of a night passage and David could see the sense in my plan. I felt that Tom should stay with his Dad and so David and I took the other watch.

Dusk set in and we began the watch system. I set a waypoint for St Catherine's Point on the southern tip of the Isle of Wight. We were 71 miles off at that time. The wind had disappeared and we plodded along under motor. Despite having some tide under us, during the three hours until midnight we only covered ten miles, not exactly racing. Just after midnight the Newhaven cross-channel ferry crossed our track, all lights blazing. I could imagine the high spirits on board, excited holiday makers on their way to France, and cars packed to the roof with camping gear and kids' beach paraphernalia. In our dark little cockpit there wasn't the same buzz. David had plenty of sailing stories to share and I could coax conversation out of Andy with open questions, but there wasn't much reciprocation. Perhaps my irritable behaviour earlier in the week had soured things.

The watch system worked well, the distant lights of Brighton slid by ever so slowly and by 05.00 the darkness had retreated. I was in my bunk when I heard the mainsail being hoisted. I crawled up on deck. Andy reported a modest breeze of 10 knots, in more or less the right direction and we gratefully turned off the engine. Peace at last. At this time it was still 33 miles to St Catherine's. The chart showed overfalls off the headland that I was anxious to avoid and this prevented us freeing off. In other words we had wind but had to sail close hauled. *Shearwater*'s slightly bluff bows punched into the channel chop and further slowed her progress.

At 06.00 I picked up the weather forecast. We could expect a south or southwesterly wind Force 3 or 4, occasionally 5 then becoming variable. There were fog patches about, just to make it more challenging. We considered and then rejected bearing away to go round the northern coast of the Isle of Wight. The tides in the Solent are a law unto themselves, four tides charge in and out each day instead of the customary two. Add to that the heavy commercial shipping movements (with huge vessels that command right of way at all times) and it didn't seem a good option. Originally I'd imagined spending a day or two on the Solent but, in reality, unless I was prepared to lengthen the time for the voyage such a plan was never going to materialise.

It took us eight hours to cover the last 26 miles to the waypoint. At one point I thought the chart plotter had broken before realising the tide was actually sweeping us backwards over the ground. In the murky visibility we could only catch occasional glances of the chalk mound of Whitecliff Bay, on the eastern edge of the Isle of Wight. The cliffs always seemed to be at the same angle to us. On the AIS I could see shipping approaching the Solent. An enormous bulk carrier was waiting for the tide to get into Southampton and was steering an erratic course, mostly towards us. I called up the bridge and she altered course.

At 14.15 I triumphantly entered in the deck log 'off St Catherine's Point. Set course for Poole.' Andy put the helm over and we eased the sheets setting *Shearwater* onto a close reach. Immediately the boat speed picked up and before long we had cleared the south western tip of the Island and in the distance to the north could make out the Needles lighthouse. *Shearwater* was racing along, like a homing pigeon on the last leg of a race. We put Tom on the helm. He'd coped well with his first night passage and never complained during our battle of attrition with the Channel tides.

I went below to consider our entry into Poole. I'd only sailed in the harbour twice before, when I'd been buying *Shearwater* and the day we left. It's incredibly popular, rammed full of yachts, but is really a vast puddle with some deeper bits around the edges. We could have anchored in Studland Bay, but were all exhausted, in need of a good meal and a restful night. I planned to take us back into Parkstone Yacht Club where they have a few visitors' pontoons. If we arrived at 17.30 I worked out it would be an hour and a half before low water. Because we were on spring tides this meant that low water would be extra low. I reckoned we had 1.2 metres of tide over chart datum (the lowest astronomical tide prediction). There wasn't much to play with. I rang Harry to ask him if there was access to the pontoons at all states of tide. He thought about it, and then confirmed we could get in. I phoned the yacht club and booked a place. All we had to do now was navigate through the shallows and moor safely.

By 17.00 we were off Poole Bay. It had taken under three hours to cover the 25 miles from St Catherine's Point. There's a song there somewhere, I thought.

How about 'What a difference a tide makes'? Tom was beaming from ear to ear when Andy relieved him on the helm. We'd all enjoyed the fantastic sail across the bay. I started the faithful engine (note the term of affection always applied when I needed it most).

Despite the approach of low water the ebb was still rushing out across the entrance bar. We gingerly edged over to the side of the channel, dodging the worst of the tide. Plenty of locals were heading home and it was straightforward to tag along in their wake. One of the questionable charms of Poole harbour is the chain link ferry which crosses the entrance. It's like a big landing craft, but on a chain. Two in fact, and these enable it to breast the fast current flowing through the entrance. It operates from early in the morning until late at night, hardly pausing for breath. When it's about to set off they run a black ball up the mast and then a flashing light shows when it's under way. Woe betides any vessel which tries to hop across its path. At best you'd get a ticking off from the harbourmaster, at worst you could be flung against the hull and rolled underneath. We tracked its course across to Sandbanks and then, together with the pack of yachts around us, shot through like a family of door mice crossing a motorway.

It was Thursday evening, the sun had chased away the fog and it was race night. Most yacht clubs hold a competition mid-week during the summer season and racing was in full swing as we entered the harbour. Everything from small single-handed dinghies to large channel racing yachts were criss-crossing the bay, sweeping round racing marks, the larger yachts frantically changing sails and hoisting brightly coloured spinnakers. We had to thread our way through this maelstrom, seeking out the correct channel which bends slowly around the outside of the harbour. You can't cut across, there's a big sandbank only just covered by the tide. David fumbled with the paper charts and didn't come up with any conclusion; I peered at the chart plotter and scratched my head. Andy meanwhile was standing on the foredeck and worked out the main thrust of the other yachts and pointed ahead. 'It's definitely this way.'

He was right. We began to pick up the port-hand buoys guarding the channel edge and made our way to the final little creek leading to Parkstone. Once there it all came back to me. Wearily we set the fenders and prepared to moor, finally tying up at 19.00. We'd covered 190 miles since we left Ramsgate some 35 hours earlier.

'Well done, lads,' I said. 'That was a hard slog.' They were all too knackered to reply, or I hope that's what it was.

Being race night the yacht club put on a decent meal that was available to visiting crews, like us. We sat in the club lounge supping pints, in a bit of a daze, then woofed down our dinner. While we ate I went through the passage plan for the next day. There was never any suggestion that we should stay an extra night. David was keen to meet up with the wives and Andy had planned to join his family for a few days' relaxation in Devon, a real holiday. The forecast was for gentle winds, probably from the south, with fog patches. Not ideal, we'd probably have to motor yet again. There was no relaxing in the bar for another pint. We headed off for our bunks and just got there before we were all asleep.

All too soon the alarm sounded and we hastily prepared to set sail. Andy went to post the marina fees and key through the berthing master's office door, David topped up the fresh water and I checked the engine. I was surprised to find it needed oil. I'd changed it in London and there was no clue from the exhaust to suggest we had been burning any. On the other hand it had been flogging along for many hours the day before. I filled it to the top marker and resolved to keep an eye on it during the day.

The crew went about our preparation without any fuss or noise. For the first time I felt we were working well together. An old hand was up and watching us from his cockpit.

'Morning, are you off?' he asked. 'You'll be heading for the Solent are you?'

'Actually no, we're off to Dartmouth.'

He paused. 'Oh, you'll be catching the foul tide at its strongest then. It floods more strongly than it ebbs round Portland.'

'Can't be helped,' I shouted. 'We need to be there by tonight.'

He looked bemused and I felt slightly uncomfortable. The whole of this week, one way or another, it felt as though I'd been banging my head against a brick wall. Whose fault was that I wondered? We cast off at 06.30, and ate breakfast under way. The ferry had not really got into its stride when we pottered past. This time the tide was with us and we motored swiftly along the channel and down to Anvil Point and the end of Swanage Bay. For the first time on the passage I was recovering my course in *Shearwater*. I couldn't claim to have completed the circuit because, of the intervention of the low-loader at Padstow, but at least from now on the waters would be familiar.

The plan was to get out into mid channel and use the favourable ebb tide as much as possible. We all knew the score when the tide turned against us, which it did early on in the morning. I set a course to clear St Alban's Ledge and to stand well out to sea off Portland Bill. From there we could sail directly across Lyme Bay to Dartmouth. During the morning we picked up a 'Pan Pan' call on the radio. This is a distress message with the status one below 'Mayday.' It concerned a missing fishing vessel, *Hope and Glory*. Peering ahead into the murky mist we could imagine all too easily the fate of a small craft suddenly confronted with a vast ship bearing down on it. Fog is probably the greatest fear at sea—well, after *The Archers* anyway.

By mid afternoon the fog began to clear and a wind sprang up, but from the west, our direction of travel. We hoisted the mainsail, bore away a fraction so as to just fill the canvas, but kept motoring. For a glorious couple of hours it backed round to the south-west before turning again to head us. The sea was calm, and when the tide turned we began to knock off the miles. David rang ahead to his marina to confirm a mooring space for us. The berthing master was a bit precious. He made us phone back and grudgingly identified a berth 'but just for the weekend, mind you.'

Tom looked up from his lap top and announced our predicted arrival time in Dartmouth. Who was I to argue with such wizardry; he was pretty much bang on, as it transpired. We would miss our rendezvous with the wives and David phoned Jan to suggest they should eat in the yacht club and we'd join them for a drink if we made it in time. I concocted a pasta dish out of left-overs and tinned food and as the sun was setting we treated ourselves to a glass of wine.

I was mightily heartened to pick up the lights of Berry Head. This is the headland overlooking Brixham, and just a few miles along the coast from the entrance to the Dart. Soon after I could make out an old faithful, Start Point Lighthouse. I fondly recalled the numerous passages back from the French coast at night when this was the leading light for the final approach to Dartmouth. On our port side the sea grew agitated. The surface was breaking as a shoal of fish panicked. Then we saw the reason why. A school of dolphins was encircling them, their tails thrashing the water to corral the fish into a dense mass before plunging amongst them to eat their fill.

The entrance to the river Dart is well hidden between steep, tree lined cliffs. Numerous rocks lurk offshore, most noticeable the Mew Stone, a good navigation mark in daylight but pretty dangerous in pitch black. To lead vessels safely into the estuary there is an isophase light (flashing in equal intervals of light and dark), in segments of red, white and green. It's a bit like landing lights for a plane. If you stray to port or starboard of the safe course you will see a red or green light. If you only see white you are home and dry (so to speak). All of this I explained to the crew, mainly for Tom's benefit.

'Tom, have you ever entered a harbour like this at night?' I asked. He shook his head. 'Well tonight you're going to steer us into the harbour. Feel up to that?'

He nodded in the cool manner of a teenager, and took the helm. The dark coastline crept by, keeping its secrets for what seemed an eternity. At last the light we were seeking winked its welcome.

'See that, Tom?' I said.

'Yep, got it.'

'Well, it's green at the moment. Keep holding your course until it turns white then, head towards it.'

Tom did the business. The castle at Dartmouth ledge beamed down and the lights of Dartmouth glowed a welcome. We moored at 22.30 having covered 362 miles in five days. Job done again.

It all felt comfortably familiar. We secured the boat and accompanied David to his yacht, *Pegleg*, berthed on the next pontoon. The two Jans were sat in the cockpit, clearly having enjoyed the hospitality of the Royal Dart Yacht Club. We climbed on board and did our best to catch up, before drowsiness overcame us. I prised Jan from the warm comfort of *Pegleg*'s saloon and stole back to *Shearwater*, where we snuggled down to sleep.

On Saturday morning Andy and Tom packed their kit. David returned for a crew photo and we said our farewells. Despite my initial misgivings, and the difficult start, the crew had once again blended to bring the boat home. I hoped they'd enjoyed it. Andy and Tom went off to find their family, and Jan and I arranged to meet up with David and his wife for meal in Dartmouth that evening. I took the mentally disturbed Autohelm to the marina engineers in the hope their electrical engineers could find the fault. After the usual teeth sucking I was told they might have time to look at it in the next few days. The weather forecast looked poor for a while so I left the unit and asked them to do their best.

During the morning the sun accidentally exposed itself amongst the clouds and we took the ferry across to mooch around the shops in Dartmouth, and then enjoyed a slow pint sat on a bench overlooking Bayard's Cove. I was pretty worn out. Back on board I had an afternoon nap before we headed back to Dartmouth with David and Jan to dine overlooking the harbour. They offered us a nightcap but I needed to be wearing one not drinking it.

Fifteen

❧

O N SUNDAY, SOME OLD OGSTON FRIENDS, Terry and Jenny, came
over from Torquay and we had a pub lunch and caught up with news. They
were heading down to Plymouth, where they berth a fine cruising yacht. We
hoped to meet up later in the week, but both suspected the weather would make
any planning optimistic. As we waved them off a familiar voice assailed my ears
with something not recordable in a wholesome account such as this.

I looked up to see my longest serving sailing crew marching down the pontoon. Geoff, Adrian and Guy are veterans from Dartmouth sailing days, survivors
of hairy Channel crossings and adventures in the Med. I had been looking forward
to this week ever since they signed up. The banter is always great and they're up
for most things. The lunch and a glass of wine had sent Jan to her bunk. When she
woke I told her David and Jan were ready to leave for home. She had a mild strop
on realising there wasn't enough time to pop back to Dartmouth to buy a fleece
she'd spotted the day before. Another shopping trip sabotaged, she was thinking,
as she stared me out. I protested my innocence. What else could I do? She packed
her bags and I walked her back up to the car and pecked her on the cheek.

'The next time I see you I expect to be back in Portishead and the voyage
complete.'

'Try and get there with the mast intact this time,' she said. Nothing like a bit
of confidence.

With the lads, I went back to Dartmouth in the evening, found some good fish
and chips and chatted through the week ahead. Our planned destination was the
Isles of Scilly but all that was in the hands of the weather gods. The forecast was
pretty lousy for the next couple of days. The guys knew the routine.

Monday morning was accompanied by rain and dense, low clouds hung over
the river, almost obscuring any view of Dartmouth. I took a load of washing to the
marina laundry and decided to check out the engine oil. Once again the dip stick

showed low. Peering down into the engine compartment I could see a black slick of oil oozing from side to side in the sump tray. I climbed into the cockpit locker from where I could access the back of the engine and squeezed my hand under the sump. There was a pipe fitted into the sump drain plug for easier oil draining. From the base of this fitting I could feel a slow drip. Got it, I thought. The only problem now was how on earth to tighten the fitting. I had all on to get my arm under the engine, let alone work a spanner. The marina engineers couldn't look at it for a few days, but lent me a small adjustable spanner and with this, and some contortionism, I managed to nip up the joint and stem the leak. I returned the spanner, and on the way back the berthing master called me into his office. I could tell from his customer-friendly delivery this was the guy who'd been underwhelming in his assistance in allocating us a berth on the Friday. He wanted me to move. We'd already moved the boat once the day before.

'I might be needing that berth for a bigger motor vessel coming in,' he said.

'Ok fine, where?' I said.

'Over on D pontoon, on the outside.'

'I'll have to wait until slack water,' I replied. In the Dart the ebb tide roars past the outer pontoons and the upriver berths are very difficult to leave without powerful engines. I recalled in my early days at Darthaven being moved to those berths and breaking a guardrail stanchion in the process.

I walked back to the boat and glanced over to the suggested new berth, amongst a row of large motor vessels. The space *Shearwater* was occupying was far smaller than any of those. He must be having a joke, I thought and ignored him. When I next saw him he said he'd sorted it anyway. Typical. The cloud failed to lift, and after skulking in the cabin all afternoon we broke out to explore more pubs in Dartmouth. The advanced party went ahead and called me to say they'd found a peach. I joined them in a classic old sailor's haunt, with low ceilings and wood panelling. The crew were perched on bar stools exchanging jokes with Gladys from Glasgow. She had them experimenting with shots and other noxious cocktails. We had planned to find another spot at which to eat but the effort seemed too great and we slunk over to the dining area and consumed a passable bar meal. I broke the news of yet another doubtful weather forecast and we retreated to the ferry dodging the rain showers.

Tuesday dawned with no improvement in the weather. 'The good natured bank holiday crowd is growing restless' best described my mates. This was not what I had planned. Devon in late July with your best sailing mates wasn't meant to be like this. There was talk of visits to tattoo parlours and other heinous distractions for bored seamen. I needed a plan.

'Right, this is what we'll do. It's not fit to venture down the coast, but we can try the engine out with a trip up the river to Totnes.' The rain was battering down on the deck. The crew looked at each other and shrugged.

'Ok, let's do it.'

I went to the marina office and paid the berthing fees. No one had looked at the Autohelm. I said I'd call back later and pick it up. We cast off and, adorned in full wet weather gear, motored up the river. In the rain and mist the upper reaches could easily have been mistaken for the Amazon basin—ignoring the absence of parrots and warmth, that is. The rain did eventually stop and the sun almost shone. We recalled previous weather-dodging trips up the Dart including one famous outing.

'This is the point where we ran aground that time,' I said.

'Ah yes,' said Adrian, 'and spent a tide sitting on the mud.'

We laughed at the memory but hadn't reckoned on an almost faithful re-enactment. We were further up the river on this occasion and one of the crew, who shall remain nameless, was on the helm. I'd gone below to put the kettle on.

'It's getting shallow,' shouted a voice from the cockpit.

'How shallow?' I asked.

'We're aground,' said the same voice.

'Oh, that shallow!' I howled and stomped back on deck.

The tide still had about an hour of flood, but for a few minutes we seemed to be stuck fast. All manner of tiller wriggling and revving of the engine didn't induce *Shearwater* to budge. Down the river I could see a motor launch approaching and, somewhat grumpily, I snatched open the cockpit locker to locate a long line.

'We'll have to see if he'll tow us off. What a performance,' I said or words to that effect.

At that moment, as if pride intervened, *Shearwater* twitched and sulkily edged astern into deeper water. The helm of the moment heaved a sigh of relief. I administered a mild rebuke for failing to spot the run of the river.

'It's pretty simple. On this side the bank slopes away slowly, on that side it's straight down. Hence that's where the deep water is.' Every one nodded as though I was telling them the obvious.

Chastened, we crept slowly on up river for a few miles but when we got to the final stretch into Totnes, the tide had run slack and the echo sounder showed scarcely enough depth. We found a spot to perform a tight turn and headed back down river. It was ironic, I thought, having navigated safely around most of the country I had managed to go aground in only two places: the first where I was brought up, and did all my early sailing, and the other where I'd kept a boat for umpteen years. Pride goes before a grounding or something like that.

We picked up a buoy off Dittisham. The sun broke through and we ate in the cockpit, now able to joke at the irony of our little adventure. The marina rang to say the engineer had looked at the Autohelm and found nothing wrong. It was ready to collect. There's nothing worse than an intermittent fault, I pondered. We had planned to spend the night on the buoy but resolved to return to Darthaven once again, to retrieve the teasing Autohelm and at least be at the head of the river, ready to spring free at the first opportunity. We berthed back at Darthaven marina and I paid over a princely sum for the 'checking.' I ruefully thought of the complimentary check over on the Tyne. Oh well this is the South coast. What could I expect?

Once again we ate in Dartmouth. The week was turning into a gastronomic survey. The crew's thoughts had already turned to their exit route home. They had booked a car hire from Penzance, having planned to take the steamer service back from St Mary's. In the days remaining, even if we could finally cast off the next morning we wouldn't reach the Scilly Isles without a nonstop passage and no one was really up for that.

We were berthed next to a boat chartered to a group of military types. Cropped haircuts, no nonsense food dispensed and eaten from billy cans, accompanied by clipped language and a steady stream of cigarette smoke. It sounds like a cruel parody but that was it. They were planning an early start the next morning and sure enough at about 04.00 I was awoken by lots of orders and thumping about on the pontoon. Clearly this wasn't to be a surprise assault.

0600 Inshore Forecast
Wind south, backing southwest or southeast Force 4 or 5
increasing to 6 in places. Sea moderate or rough.
Occasional fog patches. Rain or drizzle.

The forecast confirmed what I could just make out through the forehatch. There was a gale warning for open sea areas Portland and Plymouth. I groaned and went back to sleep for a couple of hours. After breakfast I phoned Terry, who by now was on his boat in Plymouth. He confirmed that conditions were no better in Plymouth Sound and they weren't planning to go anywhere that day.

The crew moped around the cabin, reading and joshing each other. I checked the engine oil, which was fine. At least something positive had been achieved in the last few days. I confirmed with the marina we could stay in our berth if need be. The guys went off to Dartmouth and I pottered about the boat. By mid morning the cloud lifted and the rain stopped. The wind didn't seem that strong. I phoned the volunteers who man the lookouts along the coast. They reported that conditions in Start Bay were not too bad. The visibility had improved to 6 miles and the seas had eased. Could I track down the crew? In the old days I supposed I would have run up the Blue Peter, but a fat lot of good that would have done me. I punched my mobile and was greeted by the sound of a pint pots clinking in a bar.

'We've got a weather window. How quickly can you get back to the boat?' I asked.

'We've just eaten Cornish pasties and are on the first pint. We'll be with you in fifteen minutes,' was the reply.

I hastily consumed a sandwich and once again pressed gold into the hands of the marina staff. This time, I said in the nicest possible way, I hoped not to be returning. The crew were as good as their word and within the hour we were fully kitted up and had let go. The breeze was fresh and the sea confused as we crossed the bar under Castle Ledge. It was a great relief to be under way again. We were headed for Plymouth. Needless to say the tide no longer favoured our passage and it took some time to sail across the bay and round Start Point. There is an inshore passage which closely skirts the foot of the headland, but I spurned this, as I expected the seas off the Headland to be nasty. I noticed some yachts inshore of us had taken that course. They avoided the strength of tide we were forced to punch. I suppose fortune favours the brave, but guess I prefer caution, sometimes at the expense of speed.

The seas were pretty lumpy and *Shearwater* lurched from side to side. We were able to set a deep reefed mainsail and partly furled genoa, but needed the engine to make good headway. The boat's motion combined with diesel exhaust fumes wafting across our stern got the better of Guy who promptly donated his Cornish pasty and a pint of best bitter to the fish. The poor chap went on to follow that up with most of the meals he'd consumed since arriving. At one point I thought he was even going to reveal the previous year's Christmas dinner. I tried to get him down into the cabin but he said he preferred to stay up on deck.

Off Salcombe the tide turned in our favour and after rounding Bolt Head we were able to free off and alter course directly for another Mew Stone, at the eastern edge of Plymouth Sound. Many rocks along the Devon coast share this name, which means gull. Certainly they are well covered with gull guano. All the crashing to windward had taken time. What with a favourable wind and tide would have been a passage of six hours had turned into another long flog. We were looking at an arrival late in the evening. Not for the first time I realised the consequences of setting myself such a tight schedule.

Guy was definitely not eating anything and Geoff declined the invitation, although he hung on to what he'd recently consumed. Adrian and I needed some food so I heated up a lasagne which we devoured. I prepared a list of the navigational lights for the approach up to Sutton Marina at the head of Plymouth Sound. They had confirmed a berth was available and their lock was on free flow so at least when we arrived we could motor straight in.

At the mouth of Plymouth Sound stands a long high breakwater. It does a great job in protecting the harbour from the full strength of the Channel seas, but approaching it at night is challenging for a stranger, not least of all because of the profusion of lights from the shore and around the breakwater itself. With some cunning spotting by the crew, assistance from the chart plotter and good fortune we made a safe course and slipped by the end of the breakwater at its eastern edge. A huge warship was anchored in the Sound, reminding us of the strong naval presence in the harbour. Once inside the calm waters Guy quickly recovered and helped prepare *Shearwater* for berthing. We made fast at 22.30 and nibbled some cheese and biscuits before turning in. At last the lads had enjoyed some sailing.

I phoned Terry the next morning. He and Jenny were taking their yacht Buscadeera out for a day-sail, their week's cruising having been ruined by the weather. Jenny offered to take some photos of *Shearwater* under sail so we cast off and reached down the Sound in the early morning breeze. Terry's yacht, a sleek Dutch beauty, made passing tacks and we merrily snapped each other like guests at a wedding. They veered off to anchor up in Cawsand Bay and we waved them goodbye and set a course for Fowey, a short sail down the coast. This would put us in striking distance of Falmouth, the furthest we were likely to make this week. Guy had re-arranged his car hire so, as long as we made it to Falmouth, they could get home without too much problem. Falmouth seemed a suitable point to effect my last crew change of the voyage.

We enjoyed the best day's sailing of the week. The wind was gentle, just far enough off the bow to enable us to rest the engine and *Shearwater* nudged along the coast, like a race horse cantering after a hard race. Out in the Channel the tall tower of Eddystone Lighthouse guards the rocks. The chart marks the area as a military firing range, but mercifully we were spared any orders to divert and watched from afar the manoeuvres of huge, strange looking naval ships and helicopters engaged in exercises. The radio buzzed with urgent traffic from a warship warning yachts that they were sailing into a live firing area. It's only when you spend any length of time at sea that you realise the full extent of military activity around our coast. For once we weren't 'in the way.'

Adrian pointed towards the horizon and said, 'Is that the end of the world there?'

The rest of us looked at each other and shrugged. We tacked and I noticed he'd neatly coiled the lazy jib sheet (the one not taking the strain of the sail) outside the cockpit. Not only was it out of reach for quick handling but it might be tempted to slide over the side and wrap itself around the prop. I was intrigued that after all our years of sailing there was always scope for acting weirdly. I made a mental note to increase the fresh food ration in case he was suffering from an early onset of scurvy.

Another cricket test match had started and we listened to a bit on the radio. We sailed past some sunfish, strange looking dish shaped creatures that lollop along, flopping a fin across the surface of the sea like a geriatric swimmer staggering slowly up and down the local pool. It was a fun and easy day. The beautiful Devon coastline slipped past. Looe and Polperro came and went. If the weather hadn't pinned us in the Dart there would have been time to take the ground overnight in Looe harbour, which dries out at low water. Having specifically chosen a twin-keeled boat I was beginning to wonder if I would ever get the opportunity to beach the boat intentionally. The wind freshened during the afternoon and when we arrived it was blowing strongly into the entrance of the River Fowey.

The pilot book suggested the best place to moor would be on one of the many yellow visitors' mooring buoys which have been laid on the eastern edge of the harbour across from the town quay. As we motored up towards them the harbourmaster's launch drew alongside.

'It's pretty full today, boys,' he shouted. You'll need to raft up on one of those blue buoys over there.'

'I thought the visitors' mooring were yellow?' I replied.

'They used to be. They're blue now. The yellow buoys are for locals only.'

Good old pilot book, I thought. The yellow buoys were placed snugly in the lee of the entrance cliffs. The buoys he directed us towards were rammed solid with visiting yachts, all jostling fitfully in an agitated chop. 'Find a place where you can. Don't go on those buoys opposite the quay, between the large mooring buoys.'

The harbourmaster roared off to intercept the next late arrival at the ball. We scanned up and down looking for a vacant spot. In this process you start off aiming towards the most obvious, sheltered buoys, preferably vacant and when you find these to be taken you downgrade your expectations and end up reluctantly rafting up alongside an already moored yacht. The crews of these craft sit in their cockpits giving an outward appearance of nonchalance, but exuding negative

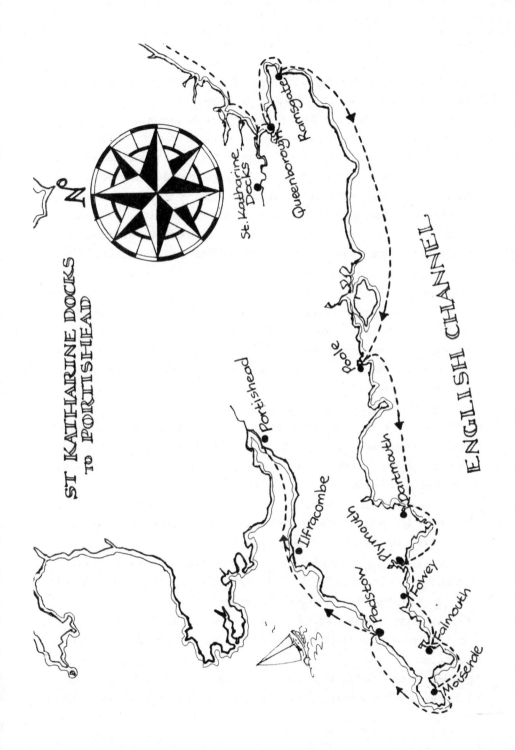

ST KATHARINE DOCKS
to PORTISHEAD

ENGLISH CHANNEL

St. Katharine Docks

Queenborough

Ramsgate

Poole

Portishead

Ilfracombe

Dartmouth

Plymouth

Padstow

Fowey

Falmouth

Mousehole

vibes to put you off choosing their boat. Etiquette dictates that unless you have a very good excuse, like the other yacht flying the appropriate signal pennant for yellow fever, you should always accept a request to moor alongside.

We motored up and down eyeing the fleet before selecting our victim. It was another Westerly, like ours, only a bit bigger. They took our lines and secured our own bow rope on the mooring buoy and positioned fenders. Their crew were friendly enough and we swapped the basics like where we were from and heading to. The confused sea didn't make for comfortable bedfellows. We began to snatch at our mooring line. This is often the case when boats of different size are moored together because each reacts differently to the wave pattern. We slackened off our bow line and that seemed to help. We agreed that it would all be better when the wind died away at night.

Originally we planned to visit the town but after a beer in the evening sun we couldn't be bothered to inflate the dinghy so I concocted dinner using a lasagne ready meal and some tinned tomatoes. I was getting adept at this, towards the end of each week. It looked as though Falmouth should be achievable the next day. We turned in at about 23.00.

Unfortunately rather than die away the wind increased and with it the sea. Our mooring was on the outside of the fleet and was catching the brunt of the swell. I tried to sleep but was jolted awake by our bow line snatching violently, followed each time by the sound of the fenders valiantly protecting our gunwale from the adjoining boat.

After an hour of this I realised we might have to move. It began to drizzle and I tried to put off the prospect of getting into wet weather gear and motoring up the river in the dark to find another berth. A particularly heavy snatch on the bow line decided matters and I put my head through the forehatch. *Shearwater* was rolling angrily against our neighbour. Each time that happened our guard rails dipped precariously towards and under his higher gunwale. I could see the possibility of them becoming entangled with all sorts of resultant damage. There was nothing for it - we had to move. I broke the news to the slumbering crew who were remarkably unfazed.

'Ok, skipper,' said Geoff. 'If we need to move let's get on with it.' Perhaps they could tell for themselves, but it was heartening that no one said 'you're jok-

ALL ABOARD!   165

ing.' We tried to untie from the other yacht as quietly as possible but inevitably their crew heard us on deck and the skipper popped his head out.

'Are you off lads?' He was no doubt relieved that he could lie more easily for the remainder of the night. We cast off and got clear without any damage. I turned the boat to head off up river, peering into the drizzle, desperately trying to muster some night vision. We motored past some large mooring buoys interspersed with still vacant visitors' mooring buoys. Whoever the harbourmaster had been keeping them for hadn't turned up. We were sorely tempted to moor up to one and turn in but something made us suspicious, so we carried on past. Geoff stared intently into the chart plotter shouting instructions as to which way the river wound. I would have used the iPad plotter but it had been playing up over the last two days and chose now not to connect with the chart plotter. I reduced our speed and stared hard at the depth sounder.

The Fowey is a deep river for the most part. Largish coasters used to regularly head upstream to the load china clay. For us it was the old nighttime challenge of working it all out from the charts. We crept around the corner of the river near Upper Carn Point. There were no visitors' buoys but there was a pontoon on the eastern shore which looked sheltered enough. Most of the yachts were moored two abreast alongside but at the end there was a solitary French yacht. No time like the present for the entente cordial, I thought.

'That's where we're going lads,' I shouted. 'We'll round up where the river gets a bit wider and head back down. Fix the fenders on the port side and get a long mooring line ready.'

The crew set to and I swung the helm over to turn *Shearwater* in a tight circle. The tide was flooding and by heading into the current and the wind we were able to nose the boat gently towards the pontoon and we brought up alongside the Frenchie with as gentle a kiss as he could have expected on both cheeks. Adrian crept across his deck and Guy hurled our long bow line across to make fast to the pontoon, and then repeated the exercise with our stern line. I cut the engine and we put on some springs. The wind was still blowing hard but there was no swell and we lay gently to our mooring. Within a few minutes we'd trooped below, discarded the wet weather gear and retired to our bunks for an untroubled night.

Friday 2 August 06.00 Inshore Forecast
Wind south or southwest Force 4 or 5, sea slight or moderate.
Showers, thundery later in the west. Visibility moderate or good.

I stirred and peered up through the forehatch. Dark, broody clouds scudded across the sky. Hardly a typical summer's day but perhaps it was in the West Country. At least the forecast looked useable and we only had 20 miles to sail, in a straight line. Needless to say our course would not be a straight line, not through any incompetence by the crew but because the wind was once again 'on the nose.' I had a sore throat and suspected the onset of a cold, hardly surprising in all the cold and rain. I roused the lads although Geoff was already up having suffered indigestion most of the night. Perhaps my 'use it all up' concoctions were at fault. I suggested we should get under way to maximise what was left of the ebb tide and eat breakfast under way. We cast off at eight. If the Frenchie slept soundly he would have been none the wiser as to his overnight neighbour.

It was damp and cold and we all wore over-trousers and jackets, together with woollen hats - typical summer sailing clothes, we joked. It was intriguing in daylight picking out the mysterious shapes we'd skirted past the night before. Just as we were leaving the pontoon a deep rumbling noise heralded a coaster nosing down river, piloted by a tug. Watching the crew manoeuvre this huge vessel round the bends of the river was somewhat humbling. We let them get clear and pottered down towards the town quay.

'Oh, my God,' shouted Geoff as we rounded the last bend. He pointed ahead to where the vacant buoys had tempted us not many hours before. Taught between the cotton reel moorings, lay a huge cruise liner. No doubt she had sneaked in at first light.

'That would have been a rude awakening,' someone said and we all felt relieved that we'd not fallen into the trap. There was barely a flicker of the net curtains as we motored past, the passengers having decided, no doubt, that a first glance of Fowey on a damp and dismal morning could wait an hour or two. After all it was hardly Venice.

The amusement and relief of what might have been entertained us for the next hour, but once outside the shelter of the harbour it was back to business. The sea was definitely at the rough end of 'moderate.' Guy swiftly volunteered to take the helm, anxious to avoid a repeat of his antics earlier in the week. The wind was fickle and the waves kept knocking *Shearwater* off her stride. He was valiantly trying to steer the boat as high as the direction of the wind would permit but this was causing her to lose boat speed and get knocked sideways by the seas. I held on as long as I could before tactfully suggesting he could do with a break. Probably more by luck than judgment, the wind backed to the south soon after and we were able to tack to clear Dodman Point and then maintain a course towards Falmouth. Adrian took the helm and made a good fist of it, overhauling another yacht on the same course. Always good fun.

The light house on St Anthony's Head marks the eastern edge of the entrance to Falmouth harbour, the largest deep water harbour in Europe. I was looking forward to returning. For once I knew the marina and its approaches. We found a tight spot on the inner edge of the visitors' pontoons and slipped *Shearwater* into place with not much more than the usual scramble and kerfuffle. The log recorded that we'd sailed 32 miles, it was probably over reading a bit but beating soon clocks up the extra miles.

The sun broke through and we ate a late lunch and lazed in the cockpit. I called up Alan, my son's former business partner, and arranged to see him some time over the weekend. It was Friday and another last night meal. I couldn't get us into my favourite restaurant, *Hunky Dory*'s, but Falmouth is awash with good places to eat and we booked into a fish restaurant near the harbour. In early evening we sat outside in the *Chain Locker*, a famous seaman's pub on the quay, then had to crowd under the beer garden umbrellas when the heavens opened in spectacular style. It reminded me of the monsoon in Asia. We made a dash for it and sampled a tasty meal. I pondered that my next 'last night' might be back in Bristol, on the very last night of the trip.

Sixteen

❧

ON Saturday morning we walked up to the square housing the Maritime Museum and lingered over breakfast in a cafe, reading the newspapers. Guy fetched the hire car and all of a sudden we were posing for crew photos on the harbour front and I was waving off another crew. I was sad we'd not made the Scilly Isles but felt at least we'd wrung a week's sailing out of a dismal patch of weather. On the subject of weather I was feeling decidedly under it. My suspicions the day before were confirmed as I began to sneeze and feel thick headed. I stuck my washing in the machine and skulked around the boat, listening to the cricket on the radio and watching the comings and goings on the pontoons.

I had the whole weekend and Monday to myself. The crewing arrangements for the last week were complicated. Jerry, an old Ogston sailor who lives most of the year in Australia, had signed up for this week to join with Dave and me on our unfinished business off the North Devon coast. After giving Jerry umpteen estimates of where I expected to be at the end of the week and finally settling on Falmouth he announced that the earliest he could join was Monday evening. To add to the complications Dave was house-sitting for some friends and couldn't get clear until the Wednesday.

So a plan finally emerged whereby Jerry would get the train to Falmouth and he and I would sail to Padstow to pick up Dave for the final passage to Bristol, via Lundy. It was just as well I didn't have a new crew arriving soon and eager to put to sea, because I was shattered, no doubt another reason why I had succumbed to a cold. I pottered into town and bought some fresh food to cook a nice supper on board. I was looking forward to a video I'd downloaded onto my iPad but that proved a failure because I set it all up only to discover the film had time-expired. I phoned Jan for some consolation then turned in early, to snuffle away the night. I slept in the main cabin, snug from the constant rain showers lashing the deck, as yet another weather front swept in from the Atlantic.

Over the next two days I amused myself, visiting the Maritime Museum, then trying to have a swim in the local leisure centre. I trudged up the hill, complete with kit, only to be told that the pool was full for the next three hours.

'I only want a swim, I don't need the flume, the wave machine or any of that stuff, just an ordinary swim,' I protested.

'Sorry Sir, we're completely full. It's red arm bands now and then there's blue and yellow to follow. You could try again at about four?' I said I wouldn't bother and walked around Pendennis Point grumbling to myself about the bureaucracy of it all. Grumpy old man's outing to the seaside sprang to mind. In the evening I began to plot the final week's passage. I read the pilots, noting all the times and schemed how to maximise the fair tides and minimise the foul currents. I'd had enough of punching the tide. I was reading too many pilot books, each with its pet theory of the best way to round Land's End. At the end of the day it boiled down to getting the right wind. A fair course with the right wind direction could make light work of the tide in most circumstances.

The wind got up again and I doubled some of the mooring lines. I turned in early to read, but then woke in the middle of the night so I made a hot drink and read some more. The rain set in with a vengeance, forcing me to completely close the companion way hatch. It was beginning to look as though the end of my trip would suffer the same weather fate as the beginning. It was no better on the Monday morning. I cleared out some lockers and cleaned the heads and the fridge (washing my hands in between). I checked the engine oil which seemed ok and decided to leave all well alone. I dismantled and re-wired the aerial from the chart plotter which had stopped talking to the iPad. This treatment failed so I packed up the offending unit and, when it finally stopped raining, walked to the post office to send it back to the manufacturer with a curtly worded letter of explanation.

To cheer myself up I decided to find a cafe with Wi-Fi and try a video phone call to my son, Fraser, in Australia. I found a place and ordered a large coffee. At first it worked well although I should have thought of using head-phones. But then a family of four came in for lunch, sat near me and each became engrossed in their separate smart phones. This fragmented the signal to the level of useless and I rang off. They were still at it when their food arrived. Don't any families talk to each other these days? I bought some food and walked back to the boat for tea and cake. I turned on the radio to find the cricket had been washed out.

Alan turned up with some beers and we had a good chat, reminiscing of old times when he was in business with Fraser. He was impressed with *Shearwater* and was soon hoping to buy his own boat. On the visitor's pontoon some of the yachts were making a dash for it, having spent the weekend waiting out the weather. One in particular, a long keeler, which are renowned for being pigs to reverse, made a good job of leaving its berth. Children in lifejackets, harnesses and anoraks festooned the decks. Ah, the joys of sailing with families. Alan set off back to his office and I walked up to the railway station to meet Jerry.

The train pulled in and disgorged the commuting workers, home from their slog in Truro or wherever. The gaggle dispersed. We're not talking rush hour in London here, just a few people. But Jerry was nowhere in sight. I thought I'd missed him but then saw a familiar figure ambling along the platform, mobile phone clamped to his ear. He walked towards me, nodded in acknowledgement and we walked slowly back to the harbour front, with him in deep conversation with his girlfriend and me tagging along looking a spare part. I hoped it wasn't going to be like this all week.

We stowed his gear and set off for the restaurant. There was a table going at *Hunky Dory*'s and a great meal and a catch-up got us off to a good start, even if Jerry was without his girl friend. Back on the boat he announced he didn't have a sleeping bag so I fished out the spare one. He has always been somewhat minimalist. On the Tuesday I awoke at 07.00 to find the deck thick with dew. Has autumn come already I wondered? I read later that in the summer this is a sign of a sunny day ahead, and so it proved to be. We topped up the water tank and motored round to the fuel berth. Someone called out my name and I suddenly remembered Alan had kindly offered to bring us a coffee and pastries on his way to work. He came aboard and we drifted about off the fuel pontoon sipping a latte and munching chocolate croissants. It all seemed very cosmopolitan for a moment. We dropped Alan off to start his day in the office and headed off towards Newlyn, our staging post before Land's End.

The wind was scarce so we motored in calm seas giving the rock-strewn coast at The Lizard a wide berth. I was telling Jerry that I'd not had a chance to take the ground with *Shearwater*.

'What about Mousehole?' he said. I could only think of the tiny fishing village along the coast from Newlyn.

'Yes that's it,' he said. 'I spent the night there once. It's a great little place.'

I left him on the helm and scurried below to consult the pilot. It confirmed my suspicion. There were no yacht moorings as such but we could dry out against the harbour wall just inside the entrance if there was room. The weather looked benign enough. If I didn't grab the opportunity now I probably wouldn't get the chance before we finished.

'Ok, let's give it a go,' I said.

We motored across Mount's Bay past the fairytale island and saw Mousehole in the distance. I looked up the telephone number in the pilot.

'Hello, is that the harbourmaster?' I asked. There was a pause and a rich West Country chuckle.

'No it's his wife. I'll put him on.'

'We can give you a night if you a want,' he said. 'When you enter the harbour turn to port and you'll see an old fishing craft alongside the harbour wall. You can moor outside him. I'll wander down and see you later.'

All I had to do now was to find the entrance. Jerry couldn't remember much so, armed with the binoculars, I squinted through the haze and studied the approach buoys on the chart. I almost got it spectacularly wrong, seeing the tiny entrance at the last minute and rounding up around a set of rocks just off the entrance. It was nearly high water, but even so the echo sounder only gave us a couple of metres of tide as we aimed for the harbour walls. The entrance didn't seem much wider than a double garage.

Once inside it was like entering another world. The sun shone brightly, kids were jumping off the harbour walls, and trippers swam up and down. The scale of everything was such that our relatively little yacht felt like an overgrown schoolboy gate-crashing the kiddies playground.

The fishing vessel was nestling against the harbour wall, a classic old timber trawler. As we drew alongside we would see it was bristling with heavy iron deck fittings. Spars lay on the deck protruding over the gunwale. The trick was to tie up securely without spiking *Shearwater* on one of its protuberances. We rigged up a fender lengthways and found the fattest specimens I had in the locker to protect our hull. We made a reasonable job of it and I turned off the engine. It felt great to be in such an enchanting spot.

'Are we going in then?' said Jerry.

'Why not? I've not had a swim all trip.'

Jerry didn't have any swimming gear. To avoid any shock to the natives I found him a spare pair of trunks and lowered the boarding ladder. The sea, having seeped into the harbour over sun-drenched sand, was almost tepid. We jumped and dived and frolicked along with the best of them, taking it in turns to pose for the camera. We dried in the sun, sipping a beer. It was just like the Med.

A young fisherman was tidying his boat astern of us. Crab pots lay around the deck.

'Any good, today?' I enquired.

'Bloody rubbish,' he said. 'It's been a bad summer for crabs and there's been no mackerel.'

'Why have you brought your pots in?'

'I'm off on holiday today. I'm missing nothing here.'

'Perhaps the crabs are on holiday too,' I quipped. He didn't reply to that. 'What are all those timbers piled up at the entrance?' I asked.

'That's for the winter, they block up the entrance. You wouldn't want to be in here in a south-easterly.'

'What happens to all the boats?'

'They pull them up on the beach, or they have to get out before they close up the harbour.' Jerry and I pondered this. With *Shearwater* nestling so gently alongside the old gaffer it was hard to envisage what he meant. Much later I saw a photograph of a huge wave breaking over the harbour wall. It made me shudder.

The harbourmaster arrived. A portly chap climbed slowly down the rusty ladder and clambered across the fishing craft.

'Good evening gents. I see you got in here alright. Staying for one night are you?'

'Yes please.' I said. 'It was a bit tight in the entrance, but I assume we'll be alright here?'

'You'll be just fine here, me boys. The sand is flat and hard. She'll settle well enough. We don't get many yachts in here. They all want showers and we've only got the public toilets up there at the end of the quay. We're hoping to get our own facilities next year.'

'How much do we owe you?' I asked.

'That'll be ten pounds.'

I paid up and he wished us a pleasant night. Jerry decided to have a shower on the boat. I found him a towel and he found the soap.

'You travel light, don't you?' I quipped. He grinned.

We changed and decided to try out the pub for dinner. The tide was ebbing but *Shearwater* had still to take the ground. The sun was still very warm and the harbour smelt salty and satisfied. We wandered around the harbour, along the narrow cobbled streets lined with tiny whitewashed cottages. A plate of grilled haddock and fine local ale added to the pleasure of the evening. The pub was heaving. I asked the landlord if it was a good season.

'It's alright now,' he said, 'But in the winter it's desperate.' A night in a cosy warm bar in the winter sounded good to me but then I wasn't trying to make a living out of it.

We just had enough room for a Cornish ice-cream and did the tourist promenade, licking as we strolled. On the public notice board there was a sign advertising the annual Christmas lights. It seemed a lifetime away but I made a mental note that it would make a delightful winter visit, without the boat. On the far side of the harbour I looked back to admire *Shearwater*, her tall mast towering over the fishing craft and day boats. I recalled how diminutive we'd felt mixing it with the vast oil-rig service ships in Peterhead and squeezed amongst the super yachts in St Katharine's. A big fish in a small pond, I supposed.

Back on board it was growing dusk. We still hadn't taken the ground and I was a bit concerned about our knobbly neighbour. From her lack of movement it felt as though *Shearwater* had touched, unlike the old fishing boat. The stout legs bolted to the outside of her hull told me she wasn't flat bottomed and relied on these supports to stop her keeling over. That was all fine provided the legs didn't sink into the sand, otherwise *Shearwater* would become the prop.

We rigged up another large fender, pushing it down between our hulls. I eyed the ugly bolt protruding from the trawler's outer leg. It would make mincemeat of our hull. Jerry was unconcerned, but that wasn't particularly reassuring. We had a coffee and sat in the cockpit watching the harbour winding down for the night. Gentle blue street lights began to twinkle amongst the cottages. I looked over the side. The sea was fast draining out of the harbour and I could make out half of *Shearwater*'s keels. I was keen to inspect the propeller, to check on barnacle fouling.

Armed with a torch I went round to the beach and paddled out as far as my wellies would permit. The water level remained tantalisingly high, still just covering the prop. I didn't want to keep returning so abandoned the idea. Back on board the old gaffer was settling on her outward leg which, as I feared, was settling into the sand causing her to lean out from the harbour, against *Shearwater*. My biggest fender was doing a valiant job but was getting squeezed to the point where I feared the tough polythene would explode. I turned in somewhat uneasy. There always seemed to be a price to pay for exploring out of the way places. I slept fitfully until at about three in the morning, when I felt *Shearwater* give a start and jerk sideways, having re-floated. She must have felt relieved to escape the pressure of her overbearing companion.

I slept soundly for a few hours but was pleased to get up at 06.00 and prepare the boat for the rounding of Lands End and the long passage up to Padstow. This would be almost a repeat of the passage the year before, but the time of the tide was slightly different and I hoped we would be able to sail up the Camel and enter the harbour without any waiting. This year we were spared the fog. There was no wind as we motored slowly back through the entrance, noting the heavy iron channels to house the timber baulks that secured the entrance in winter. We crept over the shallows outside, then when the depth sounder announced we were clear I pushed the throttle forward and *Shearwater* chugged up to her comfortable cruising speed, about 5 knots.

According to the south coast pilot (the latest version of which had been thirteen years out of date with the fuel berth in Ramsgate and the visitors' moorings in Fowey) the tide would turn in our favour off Lands End at three hours before the time of high water Dover, but when we were in line with the famous headland the readings from the chart plotter begged to differ. We had a foul tide of two knots against us and it didn't favour us for another three hours. No doubt there was some sneaky eddy close inshore, but I didn't fancy rock-hopping around the coast and stood well off to round Longships. The wind never kicked in so it was a long flog under engine for most of the day. The Autohelm overcame its nerves and held a good course, allowing Jerry and me to take watches. Jerry slept soundly during his off-watch. Despite the sun and relative warmth, he complained of being cold and stayed wrapped up in a woollen hat and fleece jacket. I hoped he wasn't going down with my cold.

We passed St Ives and he asked why we hadn't put in there. I said it was very much a drying harbour and once in there we would miss a tide and our rendezvous with Dave in Padstow. I felt as though he was enduring the passage and withdrew to my own world. During my watches I found my earphones and caught up with some music. He perked up when I made some lunch, cold meats and salad and a cheeky beer. After a long day we finally entered the Camel estuary, stowed the sails (which had done their best to contribute to our progress during the latter part of the passage) and motored into the harbour accompanied by the strains of a brass band entertaining the holiday makers.

The harbourmaster leant down over the lock gate and directed us to moor alongside a motor yacht, itself rafted up to another boat against the harbour wall. I was grateful he didn't call down and ask if we were the yacht that was dismasted the year before. I didn't want everyone to know. We tied up, ate a hastily prepared dinner and fell into bed. I was all in. The end of the voyage was in sight and with it came an increasing pressure not to mess up. Thanks to the mechanical sill the inner harbour at Padstow no longer dries out so there was no risk of a repeat of the shenanigans in Mousehole. However when we moored the skipper of the inside yacht hopped up on deck and announced he was leaving at 06.00 the next morning. I woke and helped him slip his lines, easing us alongside the inside yacht. I had originally planned to go back to bed but it was a pleasant morning and I sat in the cockpit sipping coffee.

As soon as the sill was lowered a few yachts (the late arrivals from the night before) entered the harbour.

'Morning, Rod.' I looked up to see the grinning face of Ray Williams, the engineer from Bristol, on his classic old yacht.

'Hi Ray, what are you doing here?'

'I'm on my holidays. Down to the Scillies. We anchored in the bay last night. Made it down from Portishead in one hop yesterday.'

Later in the morning I went over to see him. He was keen to hear my news of the trip. I waxed lyrical about Scotland and Orkney.

'Where are you off to next?' he asked.

'We're hoping to get to Lundy, perhaps just for the day and then back to Portishead and the end of the trip.'

'Very good,' he said.

'Can I make it back to Portishead in one tide?' I asked.

'No you won't make it back in one go.'

'What about from Ilfracombe?'

'You'll be pushing it from there. You see the strongest tide is at the end of the passage, just when you don't want to be punching it.'

I wished him well and retired to *Shearwater* to reflect. This was a bit of a blow. Because of the dismasting the year before, I'd never actually sailed to Portishead. I had assumed we could make the final passage of 55 miles from Ilfracombe in one tide, but local knowledge had just knocked that on the head. A singlehanded yacht moored up outside us. The skipper, a wild looking blond-haired chap, introduced himself as Lars, a Norwegian who'd just completed a singlehanded passage from the Azores. He'd been in the Pacific and most places in between. His yacht looked worn out but his spirit was undiminished. His self reliance was humbling. He said he was going ashore for the day to explore but he'd be back by tea time if we planned to leave then.

I walked up to the facilities and had a relaxing shave and a shower. Suitably spruced up, I took my iPad up to the harbour wall and skyped Fraser in Australia. I was close by the Wi-Fi antenna and had a great signal, much better than at home. As we were chatting a friendly voice called out.

'Morning Rod.' I looked up to see Dave, and directed him over to the boat. The crew were now complete for the final leg. We had lunch in the pub and discussed our plans. I proposed we should leave in early evening as soon as the harbour sill dropped, and anchor in a bay around the coast from the Camel estuary. We could then set off at midnight for an overnight passage to Lundy, so as to arrive at slack water, in time for breakfast. After a few hours to explore the island we would then set off for Ilfracombe to await the next flood tide up to Cardiff. From there we could head back to Portishead on Saturday, and journey's end. I was getting text messages from Jan, Bob and Marian, all keen to know if the welcoming party would be going ahead on time.

Seventeen

❦

Inshore Forecast for 24 hours commencing 18.00 8 August 2013
Wind southwest veering west or northwest Force 4 or 5,
occasionally 6 for a time. Rain or drizzle.

THE PLAN WAS AGREED. Dave and I pottered around the harbour which was heaving with holiday makers. It was three times as crowded as the previous year when we set off on our fateful passage. Jerry was going down with a cold, probably mine. He slept most of the afternoon before brightening up at the suggestion we ate ashore before departing. We squeezed into one of the pubs offering food and beat the dinner rush. After grabbing some provisions we prepared to leave. The good weather we'd enjoyed for the last few days was deserting us. Ray had decided to stay put until it cleared so I wished him well and said I'd see him next in Portishead. It was drizzling with an irritable wind pecking at the rigging. Jerry seemed pretty disinterested but when I said that Dave and I could work the boat out to the anchorage, perhaps his pride kicked in and he put on his sailing jacket.

We picked our way along the shallow creek leading from the harbour and punched the flood down the estuary and out to the sea. It was pretty lumpy and I hoped the pilot book was right in suggesting the anchorage in Port Quinn Bay would be sheltered. It was dark by the time we entered the bay and I had to rely on the chart plotter and depth sounder to get close in, to derive any shelter from the tall cliffs lining the shore. I prepared the anchor and when Dave shouted out 5 metres I let go, paying out 20 metres of chain. If we'd been planning to stay all night I'd have dropped more but we only had to retrieve it all, and according to the chart the ground holding was good. Dave ran the engine in reverse and *Shearwater* took up the slack, the chain lifting taut as the anchor bit. I leant over the bow and felt the chain. If it was dragging I would have felt the vibration. It was solid.

'We're holding. Cut the engine,' I shouted. I turned on the anchor light, a bright all round white light at the masthead. I didn't want a fisherman to run us down at this stage.

Jerry had already retired to his bunk. I set my alarm to midnight and turned in, lying in the forecabin, alert to all the sounds of the boat, the creaking of the cabin timbers, the rattling of the rigging as the wind strafed the mast, the growl of the chain shifting position on the bow roller as *Shearwater* swung this way and that at her anchor. I felt very much at one with the old lady who had cared for me so well on the trip.

The alarm woke me all too soon. The prospect of leaving a warm bunk, struggling in to full wet weather gear and sailing off into the black ought to have been enough to keep us tucked up, but this was the last chance to knock off one of the planned visits from the original schedule. The Isles of Scilly had passed us by and I knew Dave was keen to visit Lundy. Besides, once we were under way all would settle down again. At least the wind would be on the right quarter and the tide would now favour us.

I roused Dave, leaving Jerry in his bunk, while we took the first watch. It was absolutely pitch black outside. The drizzle had abated to be replaced with dense low cloud blocking out any light we might have gleaned from the moon and the stars. Dave took the helm and gunned the engine and I went forward to raise the anchor. Not wanting to bother Jerry, Dave had to go into the fore cabin to knock over the chain pile as the windlass did its work. This wasn't ideal because we really wanted someone on the helm from the moment the anchor broke free. We were close in to the shore with a fresh breeze blowing. I made the anchor secure as Dave turned the boat seaward.

Coming out into the night like this is very disorientating. I jumped below to study the chart plotter and realised Dave was heading towards a large rock at the entrance to the bay. I shouted up a course correction. It was a close one. The seas were now very lumpy. The wind felt strong, the instruments confirming gusts of 20 plus knots. It was in the right direction so I only set the genoa. Until we could get a feel of the wind strength the last thing I wanted was to be over-canvassed. *Shearwater* leapt forward and we cut the engine. Slowly our night vision improved and we could make out the lights of the coast of North Devon on our starboard side.

I checked the chart plotter again and shouted up the course to Dave.

'Steer 025° to bring up Lundy. It's 40 miles which should have us arriving around 08.00.' I suggested the same three-man watch system I'd used before and Dave turned in after an hour, bringing Jerry up on deck. He was very quiet and slumped over the companion way under the sprayhood. I stood my trick at the helm and grabbed an hour's sleep and when I returned to the cockpit the wind had freshened further and veered to the northwest. We had about 20 miles to cover to Lundy. The sea was getting up and I began to consider the anchorages ahead. The pilot book spoke of an exposed place, bullied by strong currents, and of only two tenable anchorages, on the south-east and eastern corners, very prone to swell. Yachtsmen who know it well refer to the island as 'Lumpy.'

'I'm beginning to think that it might not be a great place to anchor,' I said. 'Even though we're only planning a day visit, we need to launch the dinghy and get ashore safely. What's more, with the wind veering we'll need to harden up to make the island and we'd have to set some main.' A rogue wave hit the side of the boat showering us with spray. 'Beating into this sea won't be any fun. What say we ease off and head straight for Ilfracombe? It will be sheltered there and we can hole up during the ebb and then take the full flood up the channel?'

This met with unanimous agreement. I eased the jib sheet a fraction and set a course for Hartland Point. The pilot warned of dangerous overfalls so I set a waypoint a good two miles off. Jerry seemed very relieved. Dave came up to join me and share a brew and something from the treat box. The sky over to the east began to lighten, revealing the dark coastline of North Devon. Neither of us said anything but we both looked inshore towards the point where *Shearwater*'s old mast and sails lay rotting on the sea bed.

The wind continued to veer, and even though we'd altered course to north-north-east, I had to sheet in the genoa to bring us onto a close reach. We tracked the course of a battered old coaster heading into the channel, bound for South Wales or perhaps Avonmouth. The wind carried across the waves the sound of the steady, heavy thump of her engines. She passed us with plenty to spare. Although my watch was over I didn't disturb Jerry. He seemed out of it and in any event I was anxious to remain in the cockpit to navigate us safely into harbour. We passed Bull Point, and beyond it Horseshoe north cardinal mark guarding Horseshoe Rocks. On rounding the mark I eased the foresheet and bore away onto a broad reach towards Ilfracombe. I studied the pilot and charts, keen to form a mental picture of the entrance. We were approaching a lee shore, and there was little room for error. If we had to abort the approach we'd have to quickly turn the boat into the full force of the wind.

There was a big sea running by now. White horses hissed off the top of large rollers surging into the channel from the Atlantic. I found the telephone contact for the harbourmaster and called him up.

'Morning, we're on a yacht heading towards the harbour. Just checking if there is room on the outer harbour buoys?' I asked.

'There was plenty of room last night. I'm just on my way down there now,' he said.

'There's a good old sea running out here. Will be sheltered once we get in? This is our first visit.'

'You should be fine.'

I thanked him and reported back to Dave. The last thing we wanted was to find we had to head out to sea again. I started the engine which we left idling as we creamed towards the shore under genoa, furling it in the last hundred metres. The entrance was very hard to make out. We peered at the cliffs and buildings desperately trying to match the scenery to the harbour plan.

'There's Lantern Hill, Dave,' I shouted, pointing through the spray. He altered course and headed towards an improbable gap in the cliffs. Some breakwater triangles on poles marked a quayside submerged under high water, which didn't help. At the very last minute the harbour wall came into view and we rounded up, gratefully finding the tranquil shelter of the outer harbour. Three yachts were already occupying the visitors' buoys but there was one spare and we headed towards it. Dave went forward with the boat hook and we made fast. The other yachts seemed to be lying to a couple of fore-and-aft moorings but we only had the one. It didn't matter because the wind held us in line.

It was 08.30 when I turned off the engine. We were safe and secure, but Dave and I were all in and quickly sought our bunks. I set my alarm for two hours

ahead. Whatever our next passage plan, we had enough water under us to stay
afloat for that time and the tide would be ebbing for at least six. Time enough
to consider all that later. In the event I only slept for an hour but woke refreshed
and hungry. The lads were still sleeping like babes, albeit ugly unshaven ones. I
called up the harbourmaster who said if we were leaving on the tide we needn't
pay any fees.

'I can see you haven't got your dinghy out so don't worry.'

'Will we take the ground here at low water?' I asked.

'What do you draw?'

'1.2 metres.'

'Yes you might, we're on springs. You could move out to anchor in the pool
where that white yacht is.'

I thanked him, grateful we didn't have to go through the rigmarole of inflating
the dinghy. I took a bowl of cereal up on deck and sat in the morning sun observing the other yachts. A few dinghies were ashore, strung up precariously around
the foot of the concrete steps leading up to the quayside. They slopped about in
the swell.

'Did you come in this morning?' came a hail from a little yacht moored on the
next buoy.

'Yes, we're waiting for the tide up the channel.'

'You know that mooring buoy leads to two lines. You unhook one of them and
secure it your stern.'

'Oh, I see. Next time,' I said.'Where are you bound?'

'I'm waiting for a spare prop. This one has sheared in half.'

'Oh, that sounds expensive.'

'I wasn't surprised. I welded it together but it hasn't held.'

'Oh,' I said, amazed that such a fundamental part could or should have been
welded in the first place.

'Where are you heading?' he asked. I explained we wanted to be back in Portishead the next day.

'Are you a member of the Little Boat Club?' I explained I wasn't.

'Well you ought to come along, we meet every Tuesday. It's just down the
road from the marina.'

I felt too tired to go into a lengthy explanation about the trip, and why I lived some distance away, and didn't fancy learning how to weld my propeller together for a week or two. At the beginning of the voyage I had been eager to tell anyone who asked my plans, but somehow, having almost completed it, I felt content to keep my own counsel.

'Thanks, I'll think about it,' was all I managed. 'I'm off to work out the tides for the next passage. Good luck,' I shouted.

'You won't do it in one tide you know,' was his passing shot.

Hunger, or perhaps the rattle of our exchange had roused the babes from their slumber. Dave organised more food as I studied the tide tables and pilot. Jerry felt sufficiently confident in our salvation and arrival in Portishead,that he was busy on the phone updating his girl friend. They were due to fly back to Australia on the following Tuesday.

I finished my calculations at the chart table and announced a plan. Since the whole world was convinced we couldn't make the 55 miles passage to Portishead in one tide it seemed sensible to head for Penarth, leaving us with a short hop back to Portishead on Saturday. I didn't want to take the ground in Ilfracombe because that would waste precious flood tide waiting to re-float. I suggested we should leave shortly and punch the last of the ebb, keeping in as close to shore as was prudent. When the tide turned we could head out into the channel and take the full flood up to Cardiff. Dave was pleased that we wouldn't be ditch crawling to get into the barrier lock as we'd done three months before.

There was no dissent so we cleared up the cabin and got under way. Leaving the harbour I admired the Damien Hurst statue dominating the front, a gift from one of its most famous former residents. Yet another place I'd come tantalisingly close to seeing, but would have to visit again some day. As we turned to leave the entrance it was noticeable how remarkably sheltered the harbour was from westerly winds. The harbourmaster must have thought me paranoid to have even enquired. Our tranquil mooring quickly gave way to a hissing wall of water. The full force of the north-westerly was meeting the fast ebbing tide head-on, creating a wet and wild fracas. 'Do you mind if we pass peacefully by?' I felt like saying.

At least the wind was in the right direction. We were reluctant to set any more sail than necessary and the genoa was more than adequate. It was slow going for the first couple of hours, even the last of the ebb thwarted our progress. At no more than a couple of knots we crept along the coast espying numerous intriguing hidden coves and anchorages on the North Somerset shore. After a frustrating wait our speed over the ground crept up until it overtook our speed through the water, signalling the onset of assistance from the flood. When the tide turned it stopped fighting the breeze and the waves settled down to a long lazy, rolling swell.

We altered course to cut across the channel and bring up Lavernock Point at the entrance to Cardiff Sound. I felt confident enough of our final passage the next day to announce our imminent arrival and telephoned Portishead Quays to enquire if my berth was free.

'You're back then,' said the marina receptionist to whom I'd sent a postcard from Orkney, all those weeks before.

'Yes, we should make the early morning lock tomorrow. We're heading up to Penarth as we speak. It's a bit embarrassing but I've forgotten the number of my berth,' I said. She laughed and put me right before wishing us a good passage.

We emerged from the lock in Cardiff and I called up Penarth Marina. On saying our name they greeted me like a long lost friend. Had word spread of our arrival? The last thing I wanted or deserved was any official welcoming party. In the gathering dusk we moored up on the pontoon in front of a posh waterside restaurant that would have to forego our patronage that night. We just finished off some ready meals and dropped into bed, knowing we had an early start for the very last leg.

At 06.30 the next morning I woke and dressed quickly. I roused the lads, reminding them that we needed to make the 07.00 lock out of Cardiff. I had to chase Jerry out of the showers, I would be livid if we missed the tide. I suspected he liked to prey on my jumpiness, exuding his own version of just-in-time cool. We hot footed up to the lock which was already open and nearly full of anglers on day trips preparing their tackle.

I half-checked the forecast. It would have taken a full blown gale warning to put me off setting out on the last leg. As it happened there was hardly a scrap of wind as we motored down the Sound to join the fast lane heading to Bristol. I sang out the buoys and Dave and Jerry ticked them off. At 10.00 the familiar breakwater of Portishead sharpened its image and I picked up the radio mike.

'Portishead Marina, this is yacht *Shearwater*. Permission to enter the lock.'

'*Shearwater*, go ahead. And welcome back.'

In a flash we were through the lock and moored up. We shook hands. It was all over.

I'd travelled 2,400 miles and arrived home on the morning I'd planned all those months before. I hoisted the bunting to dress ship. Jan and the family were on their way. The party could begin.